RAINER MARIA RILKE

PICTURES
of GOD

RILKE'S RELIGIOUS POETRY
INCLUDING "THE LIFE OF THE
VIRGIN MARY"

A BILINGUAL EDITION

TRANSLATED FROM THE GERMAN AND

WITH AN INTRODUCTION AND NOTES

BY ANNEMARIE S. KIDDER

First Page Publications
Livonia, Michigan

First Page Publications
12103 Merriman Road
Livonia, MI 48150

ISBN 1-928623-65-4

Rilke, Rainer Maria, 1875-1926

Summary: A comprehensive collection of Rainer Maria Rilke's religious poetry, including the first English translation of "The Life of the Virgin Mary" in over fifty years. German and English on facing pages with the translation preserving the poet's lyrical voice and intent.

ISBN # 1-928623-65-4
I. Kidder, Annemarie, S. II. Title
Library of Congress Control Number: 2005903726

Cover Image: Ambrogio Lorenzetti (1290-1348)
Annunciation, 1344, Pinacoteca Nationale, Siena, Italy,
Scala Group, Florence/New York

Introduction

I. God

II. The Virgin Mary

*=untitled in the German original

Introduction

Rainer Maria Rilke has come to be regarded as one of the most significant poets of the twentieth century. Much of his poetry is marked by innovative and evocative imagery "painted" and conveyed through an economy of words that flow with rhythm and melody, while a frequent theme is the human heart's insatiable longing for the transcendent, the divine. In expressing this longing, Rilke had consistently drawn on two literary and artistic bodies of imagery: ancient and classical Greek mythology and the language and traditions of the Christian faith. The poems gathered in this volume have been selected on the basis of Rilke's use of language and imagery as derived from the Old and New Testaments and church tradition. They have been newly translated, with a commentary on time and place of writing and subject matter, along with the works of art, such as paintings, icons, and sculpture, that may have provided Rilke with the visual concepts for the poems' composition.

Rilke was introduced to the Christian faith through his Roman Catholic upbringing by a zealously religious, and, in Rilke's estimate, outwardly pious mother. Hertha Koenig says in her memoir about Rilke's mother, Sophia Rilke, that "the close ties with her Catholic church were so strongly apparent that one almost felt it indecorous to sit next to this woman in an earthly sphere and to have other than pious thoughts." As an adult, it is this ostentatious, outward piety that Rilke rejects as grotesque and meaningless. In its place he seeks to formulate an inward piety, modeled after the life of the saints and monastics in their direct and open dialogue with God in prayer. In this process, Rilke is aided by the artistic expressions and representations of a church that had commissioned these art works, and the regular, life-long reading of a leather-bound Luther edition of the Bible with Apocrypha.

Both the study of church art and of the Bible thus find their way into Rilke's poetry. More often than not, it is the visual representations of religious motifs that invite supplementation of detail through scriptural accounts, rather than the other way around. In this sense, the paintings of religious scenes, or religious sculpture, artifacts, and edifices originally commissioned by the Roman Catholic Church prompt Rilke to examine their related scriptural texts. The same sequence, from the visual to the verbal, seems to apply for poems drawing on paintings, sculpture, or drawings by contemporary artists depicting religious life. Rilke then adds to these visual impressions, filtered through the scriptural accounts if applicable, his personal poetic interpretation. But rather than verbally recrafting orthodox religious images in light of biblical references and interpretation, Rilke enlists these images and biblical scenes to move toward a new, at times troubling, yet at once refreshingly individualistic view of God. In this way, Old and New Testament characters grown dull from a repeated and unreflected overuse of the same attributes ascribed to them, receive a bright new coloring. Saints of the past and the present find their voices, speaking somewhat more bluntly and less confidently in matters of faith than hagiography or church authorities would wish them to. And religious artifacts and edifices gain a life of their own as they lend themselves out in service to the divine.

Through it all, Rilke constructs a glimpse of God that does not readily align with traditional church doctrine or religious creed, for that matter. Instead, his glimpse of God is so intimately nuanced and experiential that—like a personal narrative—it invites the reader to enter into the experience, to employ all of one's senses, that is, and to "taste and see." Rilke's poetry discourages a God search through intellectual analysis, scriptural prooftexting, and doctrinal consent. Rather, it prods the reader to cultivate a personal stance toward a transcendent God by extended, concentrated, and active contemplation of the visual external world for the purpose of developing an inward, authentic piety that is all one's own.

Much of the poetry's content is concerned with the quest to think out poetically the essence of prayer, the meaning of God, the destiny of the human being, and an ethics of love. The form in which Rilke pursues this quest frequently resembles that of pictures, or images, drawn not with pencil and in paint but with words that offer a concise, though highly individualistic, snapshot of an episode in the life of a biblical character, saint, or God seeker. Both form and content are interrelated and together make for what could be called a picture album of God, one to be perused at leisure and designed to evoke memories leading as far back as early childhood. These memories, in turn, may conjure up in the reader an experience and feeling not necessarily associated with a particular religion, denomination, or dogma, but one that touches upon the core of the human heart in its quest for God.

The selections are taken from the 1997 Insel Verlag edition of the 1,100-page volume of Rilke's poetry, simply titled *Gedichte* (Poems), first published in 1957 and now in its ninth edition. The collected body of poems in this volume spans a thirty-year period up to Rilke's death in 1926 at age 51, and so do the selections. I have chosen not to include poems and excerpts from *The Book of Hours, The Duino Elegies,* and the *Sonnets to Orpheus* since each book forms a unity in itself. The majority of poems selected are from five works: *The Visions of Christ* (1896/98—published posthumously), *The Book of Images* (1902/06), *New Poems* (1907/08), *The Life of the Virgin Mary* (1912)—rendered here in its entirety, and "The Completed" from *Poems 1906-1926* (also published posthumously).

The poems of this selection are grouped under five subject headings that constitute recurring themes in Rilke's poetry: The Nature of God, the Virgin Mary, Jesus Christ, Pilgrimage, and Poverty. Poems on the nature of God largely draw on characters of and scenes from the Old Testament, and are arranged in the order of the biblical books. The poems on the Virgin Mary and Jesus Christ are arranged by the chronology of Mary's and Jesus' lives based on the Gospels, Christian legend, and church tradition. The selections on pilgrimage and poverty constitute groupings that are less clearly differentiated. Under the heading of pilgrimage are included poems whose subjects are angels and members of religious orders, such as nuns, monks, and beguines, who struggle with their call of obedience to God in their journey and pilgrimage of faith. Under the heading of poverty are found poems that contrast the poor with the rich, depict saints and their implicit commitment to a life of poverty, celibacy, and obedience; and highlight the personal struggle with one's attachment to clearly defined goals, possessions, and recognition.

An overview of the individual works from which the selections are taken is intended to place the poems in the historical context of Rilke's life and thought. The works are discussed in the order in which Rilke wrote them, with the dates in parenthesis indicating the time frame during which they were composed.

The Visions of Christ (1896-98)

Rilke wrote *The Visions of Christ (Christus-Elf Visionen)* in two parts: the first beginning in October 1896 through 1897 in Munich, the second with three more poems in Zoppot at the Baltic Sea in July 1898. Following his move from his home town Prague to Munich in September 1896, Rilke had attended lectures on art history, philosophy, and religion at the university of Munich in 1897. The same year, he had moved to Berlin at the invitation of Lou Andreas-Salomé, ostensibly to continue his studies there.

All eleven Christ poems are dramatic narratives telling of Christ's role as eternal wanderer and his physical and spiritual appearance in the modern world. In most of the scenes, Christ is faced with the results of his teachings or their distortion by his followers. Several of the Christ poems, including "Christ and the Children," had been inspired by the paintings of Fritz von Uhde, whom Rilke had visited in his studio and whose work he commends in the essay "Uhdes Christus," published February 1, 1898 in the *Wiener Rundschau*. Rilke thought that the best of Uhde's work was that in which children played a role and where the painter had captured the Christ figure of love, faith, and refuge as reflected in their eyes.

In an 1897 letter to Karl Baron Du Prel, a philosopher and student of spiritualism, Rilke affirms the power of the spiritual over the material. "Every artist must struggle through the misty fumes of crass materialism toward those spiritual intimations that build for him the golden bridge into shoreless eternities." Rilke hopes to "become with word and pen one of the adherents of the new faith that towers high above church steeple crosses," so that by *The Visions of Christ*, slated for publication that same year, "I shall come a big step nearer to your group." Though the Christ poems were not published in the periodical *Die Gesellschaft*, the periodical's editor Michael Conrad played a significant, albeit unwitting, role in helping Rilke clarify his own views on Christ. Conrad, who had read the poems and had intended to publish five of them, had drawn Rilke's attention to an article titled "Jesus der Jude" (Jesus the Jew) in the *Neue Deutsche Rundschau*, detecting several similarities. Rilke was eager to meet its author, Lou Andreas-Salomé, a noted philosophical essayist, novelist, and literary critic, with whom he could readily agree on several of her conclusions on Jesus. Prominent among them was that only the loner, like Christ, "reaches the heights of religion, its true bliss and fullest tragedy; what he experiences there escapes the crowd below; his tragic end and his tragic perception remain as mysterious and individualistic as his inspiration and oneness with God—they belong outside of history." Further, she suggested that religious experience achieves validity only in living, feeling, and emphatically suffering

God solely through the emotions. In his first letter to her of May 13, 1897, Rilke recounts the essay's impact on him: "Your essay related to my [Christ] poems like dream to reality, like a wish to its fulfillment." Eventually, she would become his lover and, after their break in 1901, continue to be his confidante and the single most important influence on his intellectual and creative development throughout life.

The subject of publishing the Christ Visions was opened and closed again several times. Replying to a request of publication of the poems in a periodical, Rilke wrote to his friend Wilhelm von Scholz on February 9, 1899: "I have many reasons for concealing the Christ portraits—for a long, long time. They are gestations which accompany me throughout life. For these reasons, forgive my not yielding to your request." When asked thirteen years later by his publisher Anton Kippenberg of the Insel Verlag for previously published or unpublished poems for inclusion in a new volume of *Erste Gedichte (First Poems)*, Rilke says in a letter of January 8, 1912: I believe that "apart from the Visions of Christ, nothing usable will come of the search. And these great poems which I have not seen again for a long time, I must have about me for a while, and carry within my conscience, before they are to appear among people." As it turned out, the Visions never appeared in print during Rilke's lifetime. They were made available to the public in the third volume of *Sämtliche Werke* in 1959 and translated into English for the first time in 1967. Apart from the intimate relationship with Lou that the Visions symbolized to Rilke and possibly made him postpone their publication, he may have also felt that his readership was not ready for a depiction of Christ that called into question traditional tenets of Christian dogma. For example, in Rilke's poetry, the trinitarian concept of God as Father, Son, and Holy Spirit is missing. The doctrine of Christ's death and resurrection is reinterpreted on a personal, individualistic level, not in the context of the church as Christ's body. And Christ is more human than divine, and does not have the exclusive substitutionary role as mediator between God and humanity that orthodox church doctrine would assign to him. Thus, Rilke's Christ emerges as a unique, perennial teacher who by his human compassion, suffering, and solitude invites and models a God-search driven by feeling and an ethics of love. As a teacher, he serves in the prophetic role of confronting people with their attachments and possessions and encourages them, in self-surrender, to imitate him and the behavior of things found in creation. According to Rilke, it is through self-surrender and a childlike stance toward others and creation, not through outward doctrinal consent, that people will find themselves in a more intimate communion with God.

The Book of Images (1899-1906)

On account of only one complete English translation, *Das Buch der Bilder* has come to be known to English speakers as *The Book of Images*. Even though the German title literally means The Book of Pictures, or Picture Book, which is a more accurate description of the distinctly focused descriptive nature of its poems, I shall refer to it by its more familiar English name. *The Book of Images* evolved gradually over a seven-year period, from June 1899 to August 1906. The historical background of the book's composition is marked by great transitions in Rilke's life. It begins with Rilke's stay in Berlin and his relationship with Lou Andreas-Salomé, fifteen years his senior and married, their two trips to Russia together in 1899 and 1900, and their gradual estrangement. It continues with his stay at the artist colony in Worpswede, near Bremen, where he meets the sculptor Clara Westhoff, whom he marries in 1901, and with whom he has a daughter, Ruth, the same year. And it ends with his residence in Paris, where he moves in 1902, and in which he gradually distances himself from his wife and daughter for the sake of increased artistic freedom and productivity. In Paris, Rilke falls under the spell of the French sculptor Auguste Rodin, Clara's former teacher, who inspires Rilke's emerging poetry resembling sculptures or pictures that should eventually find its fullest expression in *New Poems*. In fact, thirty of the *New Poems* had already been written by the time Rilke wrote the last piece of *The Book of Images*, titled "The Voices," which contains ten poems of which the first is rendered here.

The Book of Images appeared twice, in very different versions. The first edition was published in July 1902, containing many poems written between 1898 and 1901 and taken from Rilke's diaries kept at Berlin-Schmargendorf, where he lived close to Lou and her husband, and those at Worpswede. The second edition appeared in December 1906 containing thirty-seven new poems, in addition to the previous forty-five, and divided the whole into two books, each with two parts. In the period between the two editions, Rilke was at work on other books as well. The third and final section of *The Book of Hours*, "The Book of Poverty and Death," was written in 1903. A second edition of the prose work *Stories of God* (first published in 1900) appeared in 1904. A novel, *The Lay of the Love and Death of Cornet Christopher Rilke*, written in 1899, was published in its final form in 1906. A monograph on the artist colony at Worpswede, in which the aspects of landscape and painting range paramount, appeared in 1903, along with the first edition of Rilke's monograph on Rodin, which was indicative of the aesthetic concern reflected in the *New Poems*. Given this diverse backdrop, it is little wonder that *The Book of Images* lacks a unifying vision of its own. In form, short lyrics alternate with dialogues, internal monologues, religious poems, ballads, and psychological portraits. In content, the book incorporates the spirituality and God quest of *The Book of Hours*, while overlapping with the sculpted images of *New Poems* and pointing beyond them to *The Notebooks of Malte Laurids Brigge*, with its feelings about the city's oppressive powers, their effects upon the poor, and God's presence among them.

Classifying and drawing generalizations about *The Book of Images* is difficult because of its hybrid quality. Commentators have frequently neglected it and the first complete, and heretofore only, translation into English of *The Book of Images* was not published until 1991. However, the book, particularly in its second edition, already shows Rilke's search for a new poetic style and an increasing distancing of the poet-observer from the object. As in a picture album, the reader is invited to gaze at or contemplate creatures and objects, including those of religious significance, or to listen in on their monologue, while the poet himself, much like a photographer or stage director, remains concealed.

New Poems (1902-08)

Rilke's *New Poems* (*Neue Gedichte*) was published in two parts, the first in December 1907 and the second in August 1908. This second part, titled "The Other Part of the New Poems" (Der Neuen Gedichte Anderer Teil), was added to the first, so that both parts were subsequently published in a single volume under that name. Rilke wrote most of the poems while in Paris and under the influence of Rodin. Those in the first part come from shortly after his arrival in Paris in 1902, including his famous "The Panther," composed in 1902 or 1903, while all those of the second part were written between the end of July 1907 and the middle of August 1908.

The *New Poems* were aptly called new by Rilke for they mark a distinct new phase in Rilke's creativity. This creativity was closely linked with Rodin, on whose account he had moved to Paris so as to write the sculptor's monograph. The monograph was published the following year, 1903, and again in an expanded edition in 1907, so that Rilke had the time to devote himself to his poetic craft. Propelled by Rodin's watch word to seize the day with work (*Il faut tojour travailler*) and the desire to imitate the sculptor's rigorous and indefatigable work routine, Rilke begins looking for ways to use his poetic talent in a continuous flow of creative output. Like the sculptor, he trains his eye to intensely observe and concentrate on a random object and then to render poetically its visual features and movements in distinct and densely packaged fashion. What results has come to be known as the object poem, or "Ding-Gedicht," focusing on a single object, be it flower, animal, statue, edifice, or human being. With the object poem, Rilke then had found a way to set to work immediately and systematically. By 1906, he had compiled a list of more than a hundred titles, or subjects, for poems, and upon its completion drew a line through the listed title and appended a date.

In their form, the *New Poems* mark a departure from Rilke's previous poetry, most notably from the lyrical and narrative quality of the poem prayers in *The Book of Hours*. The individual poems form self-contained units, each with its own title, and each describing and observing an object, animal, person, or scene. As a result no line or phrase has any independent value and significance, or would lend itself to being quoted out of context and apart from the whole. In her 1935 book *Rainer Maria Rilke: Ein Kommentar*, Katharina Kippenberg, the wife of Rilke's publisher and her husband's collaborator, notes the similarity of *New Poems* to sculptures. The poems' words "are chiseled by the manliest of hands and their verses are so three-dimensional that one has the feeling one can walk about and touch" things in them. "There is nothing imprecise, each part is given equal justice as would the sculptor." Moreover, the poems resemble great sculptural masterpieces by their "being totally occupied with themselves" without any reference to the observer (104-5).

Rilke's *New Poems* also marked a new turn in the history of German literature. According to the Austrian novelist Robert Musil in a lecture delivered a few weeks after Rilke's death in 1927, it was Rilke who with his *New Poems* first brought the German short poem to perfection. While Goethe, for example, had often been content to fill out poems containing a few exquisite lines or stanzas with undistinguished, random loquacity, Rilke taught Germans again what a poem was. The British scholar J. B. Leishman, who for several decades held the monopoly on translating Rilke into English, concurs with Musil, but goes one step further: *New Poems*, he says in his introduction of his translation of the work, was not only new to German poetry, but "new to European poetry" in the poems' form, elegance, and concentration of words and images (3). With the object poem Rilke seems to have anticipated the new developments of the Imagist group of the twentieth century, begun by a group of poets in London in the years prior to 1913, and popularized in the United States. The guidelines for writing poetry employed by the group's adherents resemble Rilke's approach: they proposed to present sharp and precise images, use the language of common speech, create new rhythms to express new moods (usually using free verse), allow for freedom in the choice of the subject matter, and strive for concentration by avoiding unnecessary words and phrases. The London group had been inspired by the American poet Ezra Pound and was eventually championed in both England and the United States under the leadership of the American poet Amy Lowell. Lowell, whose first book of poems was published in 1910, and who had joined the Imagist group in 1913, was awarded a Pulitzer prize for a volume of poems in 1925, shortly after her death.

Following the publication of the 1908 edition of *New Poems*, Rilke was working on yet another, a third part of *New Poems*, which he hoped would surpass the previous two. In a letter written on August 18, 1908 to his publisher, Anton Kippenberg, Rilke regards the other, second part of *New*

Poems as having been composed at "a greater depth and with more distance" than the first. "If a third volume is to join these two, a similar intensification will still have to be achieved in that ever more objective mastering of reality, out of which emerges, quite spontaneously, the wider significance and clearer validity of all things." It is likely that several of the poems written that year and the next were intended for the third part of *New Poems*. However, Rilke may have grown tired of continuing in the same vein of writing, so that the third part never appeared. Instead, poems patterned after *New Poems* and probably written for the third part were never specifically identified by Rilke and thus went into the body of literary papers found after his death. These so-called uncollected poems were published posthumously as *Poems 1906 to 1926 (Gedichte 1906 bis 1926)*. The first and largest of the three-partite work of *Poems 1906 to 1926*, is titled "The Completed" ("Vollendetes") and probably contains several poems Rilke had initially written for *New Poems'* third part.

The Life of the Virgin Mary (1912)

Rilke wrote *The Life of the Virgin Mary (Das Marien-Leben)* during the week of January 15 to 22, 1912 in Duino, Italy. Rilke had been staying there between October 22, 1911 to May 9, 1912, with some interruptions, at its castle owned by the Austrian-born Princess Marie of Thurn and Taxis-Hohenlohe. It is at this castle that only weeks after completing the Mary poems, he also writes the first two of the ten so-called *Duino Elegies*, which should not be completed until 1922.

The Life of the Virgin Mary is a series of thirteen poems describing the life of the Virgin Mary, based on the Gospel accounts and Christian legend. The poems mark a midpoint between Rilke's publication of the second part of *New Poems* in 1908 and the final and sudden "appearance" of the rest of the *Duino Elegies* and the *Sonnets to Orpheus* in 1923 at Muzot, Switzerland, prior to his death in 1926. It is said that the intense labor on the prose work *The Notebooks of Malte Laurids Brigge*, begun in 1904 and finished in 1910, had exhausted Rilke to such a degree that he found himself directionless until his final creative output in 1923. As a result, the years from 1910 through 1922 have often been portrayed as Rilke's crisis years, so that generally little attention has been afforded to his literary output during that time. This is especially true for the *Life of the Virgin Mary*, whose most recent translations into English date back to the nineteen-forties (C.F. MacIntyre, 1947) and fifties (Stephen Spender, 1951).

During the years of 1910 through 1922, Rilke had been writing continuously—in letters, in guest books, and above all, in the pocket-books he always carried. In fact, the source of Rilke's *The Life of the Virgin Mary* was the notations he had entered in the guest book of a close friend and then well-known Judendstil artist, Heinrich Vogeler, at the artist colony in Worpswede. Rilke had first met Vogeler in the spring of 1898 in Florence, and visited and stayed with him at the Barkenhoff several times over the next two years. Vogeler's Barkenhoff at Worpsede had become a center of intellectual and cultural life in Germany, with prominent, regular house guests that included the writers Carl and Gerhart Hauptmann and the director Max

Reinhardt. In 1903, Rilke had published a monograph on Worpswede, describing several of the painters and their work at the colony, including Vogeler's. Rilke returned to Worpswede in 1903 and, again, in 1905, where he worked on the proofs of *The Book of Hours* and consulted with Vogeler on the book's graphic design. After a hiatus in their relationship, Rilke met Vogeler again in Paris in 1911, whereupon the latter was moved to revive an old plan of theirs, namely producing an illustrated poetry cycle of the life of Mary. Vogeler then inquired with Rilke's publisher, Anton Kippenberg, who told Rilke of Vogeler's plan in a letter sent to Duino. In his reply to Kippenberg on January 1912, Rilke is skeptical about the project since over the years he had "lost touch with [Vogeler's] work, much in the same way as what I am doing now is probably totally eluding him as well" (*Briefe an seinen Verleger,* 156). However, Rilke has his publisher send him the ten Mary poems Vogeler had been referring to, contained in the manuscript titled *In und Nach Worpswede* (*At Worpswede and Thereafter*). To his surprise, "there are several beautiful ones among them that still deeply touch me," he writes to Kippenberg; "but they are not sufficient" for a cycle on the Virgin Mary (*Briefe and seinen Verleger,* 161). Rilke is probably referring to the two poems "Annunciation to Mary" and "Stop on their Flight to Egypt," which Rilke had written immediately after Vogeler had shown him sketches drawn of these biblical scenes in September 1900. Instead, Rilke suggests to compile and edit the entire Worpswede manuscript and have Vogeler do the art work. But something unexpected happens: moved by the reading of the old manuscript from his days at Worpswede, Rilke composes at least ten new Mary poems in a week's period, which would soon become one of the poet's best known works.

Indebted to the painter for the new inspiration, Rilke feels obliged to allow Vogeler to draw sketches for the new Mary poems. When the sketches are sent to the publisher, Vogeler expresses concern about them. Rilke, too, finds that the sketches do not match the poetry and so decides to publish the Mary cycle without any illustrations. As a consolation to his friend, Rilke dedicates the volume of poems to Vogeler "so as to at least remain in memory close to our former plan and to be with him united within the book" (*Briefe an seinen Verleger,* 183). The dedication reads: "To Heinrich Vogeler with gratitude for the former and new occasion of these verses."

In the composition of the Mary poems Rilke recognizes the resurgence of a newly flowing creativity. When sending the poems off for publication, Rilke describes them in his note to Katharina Kippenberg as "the small mill of the Life of the Virgin Mary" that had been spun about by the underlying torrent of the *Elegies.* Concurrently, he adds to *The Life of the Virgin Mary* a Greek subtitle that translates as "Having a storm within." On June 1, 1922 in a letter to Countess Sizzo, he gives credit for his inspiration of the Mary cycle to the Italian and Russian masters. For "much of the details and the order of this picture series is not my own invention" and one would be hard pressed not to recognize "in the climb of the little girl Mary up to the temple," for example, the pictures of Italians, such as Tizian or Tintoretto; all other times, "I am vastly indebted to and have been inspired by the famous recipe book of all paintings of saints, The Painter's Handbook of Mount Athos

[1855], and even the so-called Kiewski Paterik (an orthodox Russian collection of suggestions and instructions for the depiction of biblical objects)." Henceforth, *The Life of the Virgin Mary* is the only complete work of Rilke's that was ever set to music. In 1923, Paul Hindemith wrote the first version, followed by a second one in 1948, for soprano voice and piano. This volume includes the entire cycle of Mary poems.

Poems 1906 to 1926

The poems contained in *Poems 1906 to 1926* stem from the literary body of papers found after Rilke's death in 1926 and comprise the work of those years. They are only those written in German and exclude the more than 450 poems Rilke wrote in French between 1923 and 1926. Except for a few that had appeared in the journal *Insel-Almanach* and other periodicals during Rilke's lifetime, these poems written in the German language had not been collected and published in book form by Rilke himself. Because of this, the poems are frequently referred to in the English-speaking world as Rilke's "uncollected poetry." The term was coined by J. B. Leishman, whose complete translation of them appeared in 1957, following the first German edition published as late as 1953 by Insel Verlag and edited by Ernst Zinn.

To judge from the poems' sheer quantity, Rilke had grown more and more indifferent to publication during the twenty-year period preceding his death. There are over five hundred pieces, ranging from completed poems, to mere statements about their subjects and fragments, to pithy sayings and aphorism, dedicatory poems, monologues, and elegies.

The German edition distinguishes these poems by type and divides them into three sections: "The Completed" (*Vollendetes*), "Dedications" (*Widmungen*), and "Drafts" (*Entwürfe*). In his 1964 English translation, Leishman follows the chronological order of their writing, instead, based on the dates added by Rilke himself or by reconstructing the dates and places of composition—and sometimes even the occasion that prompted their writing—from Rilke's pocket-books; from his inscriptions in books, albums, and guest books; and from manuscript copies given to friends. This fastidious scholarship, more so perhaps than the translation itself, has contributed enormously to tracing Rilke's creative output and development in his later years beginning with the year 1906.

That the collection should commence in 1906 might involve the year's significance as a time of new beginnings. Rilke had completed the transition from the publisher of his earlier works, Axel Juncker, to Anton Kippenberg's Insel Verlag: *The Book of Images* is still published with Juncker, while *The Book of Hours,* first published in 1905, and all his later works appear with the Insel Verlag. Rilke had also embarked on a new approach to work: he had begun to systematically compose poems, to be published in 1907 and 1908 as *New Poems*. This systematic approach to work, as well as the poems' form as so-called object poems, was new. The year also marks the break with Rodin in May, precipitated by a letter Rilke had answered when serving as private secretary to the sculptor without consulting the latter. This break ended Rilke's own voluntary subordination to Rodin. It freed up his time again, offered in exchange for Rodin's hospitality, to give undivided attention to his own work, while moving out of Rodin's house freed him from the sculptor's dominating influence. At the same time, Rilke moved that year from his study of sculpture back to painting, most prominently the paintings of the Frenchman Paul Cézanne. When later asked by Alfred Schaer of the University of Zürich what had been among the chief influences on him and his work, Rilke replied in a letter of February 26, 1924, that since 1906, there had stood before him as "the most powerful influence" (*als das stärkste Vorbild*) the work of Cézanne, who had died the same year.

Leishman's remains the only complete English translation of *Poems 1906 to 1926*. In 1996, Edward Snow published a selection, titled *Uncollected Poems*, which follows the same chronological order. All poems stemming from this period and contained here, with the exception of "Elegy of a Nun" ("*Nonnenklage*," 1909), "Moses's Death (*"Der Tod Moses*," 1915), and "Imaginary Curriculum Vitae" ("*Imaginärer Lebenslauf*"), were written in 1913, shortly after Rilke had completed the Mary cycle.

Bibliography

Exner, Richard. Vorwort in Rainer Maria Rilke, *Das Marien-Leben*. Introd. by Richard Exner. Frankfurt: Insel Verlag, 1999.

Holthusen, Hans Egon. *Rainer Maria Rilke: Mit Selbstzeugnissen und Bilddokumenten*. Hamburg: Rowohlt Verlag, 1958.

Kippenberg, Katharina. *Rainer Maria Rilke: Ein Beitrag*. Leipzig: Insel Verlag, 1935.

Koenig, Hertha. *Rilkes Mutter*. Tübingen: Neske Verlag, 1963.

Leishman, J. B. "Introduction" in Rainer Maria Rilke. *New Poems*. Translation and Notes by J. B. Leishman. London: The Hogarth Press, 1964.

_____. "Introduction" in Rainer Maria Rilke. *Poems 1906 to 1926*. Trans. J. B. Leishman. London: The Hogarth Press, 1957.

Mandel, Siegfried. Introduction in Rainer Maria Rilke. *Visions of Christ: A Posthumous Cycle of Poems*. Introduction Siegfried Mandel. Trans. Aaron Kramer. Boulder: University of Colorado Press, 1967.

Metzger, Erika A. and Michael M. Metzger. *A Companion to the Works of Rainer Maria Rilke*. Rochester, NY: Camden House, 2001.

Musil, Robert. *Tagebücher, Aphorismen, Essays und Reden*. 1955.

Pettit, Richard. *Rainer Maria Rilke in und um Worpswede*. Worpswede: Worpsweder Verlag, 1983.

Rilke, Rainer Maria. *Briefe an seinen Verleger 1906 bis 1926*. Eds. Ruth Sieber-Rilke and Carl Sieber. Leipzig: Insel Verlag, 1934.

_____. *Werke: Kommentierte Ausgabe in Vier Bänden*. Eds. Manfred Engel, Ulrich Fülleborn, Horst Nalewski, August Stahl. Frankfurt: Insel Verlag, 1996.

Rilke, Rainer Maria, and Lou Andreas-Salomé. *Briefwechsel*. Ed. Ernst Pfeiffer. Zürich: M. Niehaus, 1952.

Schnack, Ingeborg. *Rainer Maria Rilke: Chronik seines Lebens und Seines Werkes*, 2 vols. Frankfurt: Insel Verlag, 1975.

Snow, Edward. Introduction in Rainer Maria Rilke. *The Book of Images*. Trans. Edward Snow. San Francisco: North Point Press, 1991.

Snow, Edward. Introduction in Rilke, Rainer Maria. *Uncollected Poems*. Selected and trans. by Edward Snow. New York: North Point Press, 1996.

PICTURES OF GOD:

RILKE'S RELIGIOUS POETRY
INCLUDING
"THE LIFE OF THE VIRGIN MARY"

I. Gott

Gott am Werk*

Du darfst nicht warten, bis Gott zu dir geht
und sagt: Ich bin.
Ein Gott, der seine Stärke eingesteht,
hat keinen Sinn.
Da mußt du wissen, daß dich Gott durchweht
seit Anbeginn,
und wenn dein Herz dir glüht und nichts verrät,
dann schafft er drin.

Gott im Mittelalter

Und sie hatten Ihn in sich erspart
und sie wollten, daß er sei und richte,
und sie hängten schließlich wie Gewichte
(zu verhindern seine Himmelfahrt)

an ihn ihrer großen Kathedralen
Last und Masse. Und er sollte nur
über seine grenzenlosen Zahlen
zeigend kreisen und wie eine Uhr

I. God

God at Work*
(In Celebration of Me, 1898)

Don't expect that God will come up to you one day
and say, Here I am.
A God who admits to his own strength
wouldn't make much sense.
You need to realize that God has been throbbing
from the start through your entire core,
and when your heart is aglow and will not say why,
that's when God is at work.

With few exceptions Rilke wrote Mir Zur Feier (In Celebration of Me) between early November 1897 and the end of May 1898 in Berlin, Arco, Florence, and Viareggio. It was published in a first edition in 1898/99 and in a second, final edition in 1908/09. The book's title implies the celebration of a future "Me," which aspires to distill the true self in relation to God from a painful childhood, traditional conventions, the status quo, and the otherworldly consolations and detachments of the Christian religion. The above poem is untitled in the original and is the last one in Mir Zur Feier. Viareggio, May 1898.

God in the Middle Ages
(New Poems, 1907)

Only for themselves they had saved up God
and wanted him to exist and to judge,
and they hitched unto him like heavy weights
(to prevent his escaping heavenward)

their huge cathedrals as burden and mass.
For God only was supposed to be running
in circles around the endless numerals
like a clock.

Zeichen geben ihrem Tun und Tagwerk.
Aber plötzlich kam er ganz in Gang,
und die Leute der entsetzten Stadt

ließen ihn, vor seiner Stimme bang,
weitergehn mit ausgehängtem Schlagwerk
und entflohn vor seinem Zifferblatt.

Imaginärer Lebenslauf

Erst eine Kindheit, grenzenlos und ohne
Verzicht und Ziel. O unbewußte Lust.
Auf einmal Schrecken, Schranke, Schule, Frohne
und Absturz in Versuchung und Verlust.

Trotz. Der Gebogene wird selber Bieger
und rächt an anderen, daß er erlag.
Geliebt, gefürchtet, Retter, Ringer, Sieger
und Überwinder, Schlag auf Schlag.

Und dann allein im Weiten, Leichten, Kalten.
Doch tief in der errichteten Gestalt
ein Atemholen nach dem Ersten, Alten. . .

Da stürzte Gott aus seinem Hinterhalt.

He should mark off their labor and daily chores.
But, instead, all at once he took off
and the people in town were beside themselves,

and let go of him—scared by his voice and ways,
to run on his own with the clockwork exposed;
and they ran from his, the clock's, face.

Paris, July 19-23, 1907

Imagined Curriculum Vitae
(Poems 1906-1926)

First a childhood, so limitless, no need,
no goal. O pleasure one does not perceive.
Then all at once fright, barrier, duty, school
and a collapsing with temptation, loss.

Spite. The once plied becomes the one who plies
and takes revenge on others when succumbed.
Loved, feared, savior, wrestler, victor
and conqueror, one by one.

And then alone amidst the vastness, lightness, cold.
But deep within the one who stands erect
there is an inhaling of the Beginning One, the Old . . .

Then God breaks forth from back.

Written at the request of Forest Inspector Burri for the Festschrift of the Free Association of Like-Minded in Lucerne; Schöneck, September 15, 1923.

Adam

Staunend steht er an der Kathedrale
steilem Aufstieg, nah der Fensterrose,
wie erschreckt von der Apotheose,
welche wuchs und ihn mit einem Male

niederstellte über die und die.
Und er ragt und freut sich seiner Dauer
schlicht entschlossen; als der Ackerbauer
der begann, und der nicht wußte, wie

aus dem fertg-vollen Garten Eden
einen Ausweg in die neue Erde
finden. Gott war schwer zu überreden;

und er drohte ihm, statt zu gewähren,
immer wieder, daß er sterben werde.
Doch der Mensch bestand: sie wird gebären.

Eva

Einfach steht sie an der Kathedrale
großem Aufstieg, nah der Fensterrose,
mit dem Apfel in der Apfelpose,
schuldlos-schuldig ein für all Male

an dem Wachsenden, das sie gebar,
seit sie aus dem Kreis der Ewigkeiten
liebend fortging, um sich durchzustreiten
durch die Erde, wie ein junges Jahr.

Adam
(Of the New Poems' Other Part, 1908)

Amazed he stood by the towering cathedral
near the rose window
as if shaken by the apotheosis
that had evolved and had suddenly placed

him above this one and that.
And he towers delighted at his enduring
survival as the farmer who had begun,
and didn't know how,

to plow an exit to the new earth
away from Eden that had stood complete.
God was hard to persuade

and threatened to allow, in turn,
man to commence the cycle of death.
But man insisted: she will give birth.

Paris, summer 1908

Eve
(Of the New Poems' Other Part, 1908)

Unpretentiously she stood by the towering cathedral
near the rose window
with the apple in the apple pose
innocently guilty henceforth

of what would grow in her, what she would bear,
since she had left the beloved
land of eternity so as to contend
with the earth, like a new year.

Ach, sie hätte gern in jenem Land
noch ein wenig weilen mögen, achtend
auf der Tiere Eintracht und Verstand.

Doch da sie den Mann entschlossen fand,
ging sie mit ihm, nach dem Tode trachtend;
und sie hatte Gott noch kaum gekannt.

Ein Prophet

Ausgedehnt von riesigen Gesichten,
hell vom Feuerschein aus dem Verlauf
der Gerichte, die ihn nie vernichten,—
sind die Augen, schauend unter dichten
Brauen. Und in seinem Innern richten
sich schon wieder Worte auf,

nicht die seinen (denn was wären seine
und wie schonend wären sie vertan)
andre, harte: Eisenstücke, Steine,
die er schmelzen muß wie ein Vulkan,

um sie in dem Ausbruch seines Mundes
auszuwerfen, welcher flucht und flucht;
während seine Stirne, wie des Hundes
Stirne, das zu tragen sucht,

was der Herr von seiner Stirne nimmt:
Dieser, Dieser, den sie all fänden,
folgten sie den großen Zeigehänden,
die Ihn weisen wie Er ist: ergrimmt.

O how she would have enjoyed
to stay a little longer in this place
and watch the animals' harmony and thought.

But since she found the man was set,
she followed him into pursuing death,
though having barely known God.

Both poems on Adam and Eve were inspired by the two nineteenth-
century sculptures by Viollet-le-Duc on the west front facade of the
Cathedral of Notre Dame; Paris, summer 1908.

A Prophet
(Of the New Poems' Other Part, 1908)

His eyes are wide with massive sights,
aflame with the fires of various courts
that never laid a hand on him,—
below bushy brows they rest.
And from within him there already arise
newly created words,

not his own (for they would be
way too mild, hence a waste)
but others, so hard: blocks of iron, slabs,
the volcano in him had to melt

and hurl with the force of his tongue
as a stream of curses and bans;
and his head is willing to bear,
like that of a dutiful dog,

what would otherwise befall the Lord's:
and they all would be able to find the One, Him
if only they heeded these hands outlining
the way He is: grim.

Der Tod Moses

Keiner, der finstere nur gefallene Engel
wollte; nahm Waffen, trat tödlich
den Gebotenen an. Aber schon wieder
klirrte er hin rückwärts, aufwärts,
schrie in die Himmel: Ich kann nicht!

Denn gelassen durch die dickichte Braue
hatte ihn Moses gewahrt und weitergeschrieben:
Worte des Segens und den unendlichen Namen.
Und sein Auge war rein bis zum Grunde der Kräfte.

Also der Herr, mitreißend die Hälfte der Himmel,
drang herab und bettete selber den Berg auf;
legte den Alten. Aus der geordneten Wohnung
rief er die Seele; die, auf! und erzählte
vieles Gemeinsame, eine unzählige Freundschaft.

Aber am Ende wars ihr genug. Daß es genug sei,
gab die vollendete zu. Da beugte der alte
Gott zu dem Alten langsam sein altes
Antlitz. Nahm ihn im Kusse aus ihm
in sein Alter, das ältere. Und mit Händen der Schöpfung
grub er den Berg zu. Daß es nur einer,
ein wiedergeschaffener, sei unter den Bergen der Erde,
Menschen nicht kenntlich.

Possibly based on Michelangelo's depiction of prophets in the Sistine Chapel. The prophet described may have been Ezekiel to whom the Lord appeared surrounded by fire and as the punishing Lord of Judgment of a stubborn people. Paris, August 1907.

Moses's Death
(Poems 1906-1926)

None of the angels, but the dark and fallen one
was willing; took up arms and with deadly intent
approached the one to whom he had been sent.
But again he rattled away, backwards, and up
to the heavens he screamed: I can't.

For nonchalantly through the heavy brow
Moses had seen him coming and continued to write:
words of blessing and the everlasting name.
And his eye was pure to the depth of his core.

Thus, the Lord himself, carrying along half the heavens
came down and removed the covers of the hill like a bed;
placed the old man there. And from this well-ordered house,
he called the soul forth to rise, up! to recount
the many common things of a friendship deeply laid.

And in the end, the soul had enough, was satisfied,
and said this much. Then, the ancient God
bent toward the old man His old face and took
life with a kiss out of him into His own,
the older one. And with the hands of creation
He covered the mountain so as to disguise
it as one among many others
and to keep it from being recognized.

Deuteronomy 34; Paris, summer 1914 and Munich, October 1915

Josuas Landtag

So wie der Strom am Ausgang seine Dämme
durchbricht mit seiner Mündung Übermaß,
so brach nun durch die Ältesten der Stämme
zum letzten Mal die Stimme Josuas.

Wie waren die geschlagen, welche lachten,
wie hielten all Herz und Hände an,
als hübe sich der Lärm von dreißig Schlachten
in einem Mund; und dieser Mund begann.

Und wieder waren Tausende voll Staunen
wie an dem großen Tag vor Jericho,
nun aber waren in ihm die Posaunen,
und ihres Lebens Mauern schwankten so,

daß sie sich wälzten von Entsetzen trächtig
und wehrlos schon und überwältigt, eh
sie's noch gedachten, wie er eigenmächtig
zu Gibeon die Sonne anschrie: steh:

Und Gott ging hin, erschrocken wie ein Knecht,
und hielt die Sonne, bis ihm seine Hände
wehtaten, ob dem schlachtenden Geschlecht,
nur weil da einer wollte, daß sie stände.

Und das war dieser; dieser Alte wars,
von dem sie meinten, daß er nicht mehr gelte
inmitten seines hundertzehnten Jahrs.
Da stand er auf und brach in ihre Zelte.

Er ging wie Hagel nieder über Halmen:
Was wollt ihr Gott versprechen?

Joshua's Farewell
(New Poems, 1907)

Just like the river at its dams
breaks through the gate with might,
that's how the voice of Joshua
rings through the ancients' tribes.

How were they slapped who laughed at first;
how did they halt their heart and hand,
as if the noise of thirty wars
rose in one mouth, which now began.

Again the thousands were amazed
like on that day at Jericho,
but in it blew the trumpets now
and their lives' walls were trembling, so

they rolled about like terrorized,
without defense, were overrun,
before they could remember how
at Gibeon he'd stopped the sun;

And God went, like a servant afraid,
and held up the sun, His hands ached
on account of this murderous mob,
because one wanted the sun to stop.

And the one was he, this old man,
who at the age of a hundred and ten
they thought held no longer his own.
There he rose and swept through their tents.

He came down like hail over blades of grass:
What do you want to promise God?

Ungezählt stehn um euch Götter,
wartend daß ihr wählt.Doch wenn ihr wählt,
wird euch der Herr zermalmen.

Und dann, mit einem Hochmut ohnegleichen:
Ich und mein Haus, wir bleiben ihm vermählt.

Da schrien sie alle: Hilf uns, gieb ein Zeichen
und stärke uns zu unserer schweren Wahl.

Aber sie sahn ihn, wie seit Jahren schweigend,
zu seiner festen Stadt am Berge steigend;
und dann nicht mehr. Es war das letzte Mal.

Saul unter den Propheten

Meinst du denn, daß man sich sinken sieht?
Nein, der König schien sich noch erhaben,
da er seinen starken Harfenknaben
töten wollte bis ins zehnte Glied.

Erst da ihn der Geist auf solchen Wegen
überfiel und auseinanderriß,
sah er sich im Innern ohne Segen,
und sein Blut ging in der Finsternis
abergläubig dem Gericht entgegen.

Wenn sein Mund jetzt troff und prophezeite,
war es nur, damit der Flüchtling weit

Many are the gods from whom to choose,
that press about. And if you did, the Lord
would grind you down.

And then, with unprecedented pride, they said:
I and my house to Him we'll stay wed;

and then they cried: help us, give us a sign
and strengthen us in this our weighty pact.

Instead they saw him silent, as these years before,
ascending to his fortressed city up the hill:
and then no more.

*Joshua 24; at Joshua's request God had stopped the sun and the moon
for the battle of the Israelites against the Amorites (Joshua 10:12ff).
The sentence "since the Lord obeyed the voice of a man" is marked in
Rilke's Bible. Paris, July, 1906*

Saul Among the Prophets
(Of the New Poems' Other Part, 1908)

Do you presume to see yourself sinking low?
No, the king still thought himself in power
since he devised to kill his servant boy
playing the harp, to the tenth degree.

Only when during such stratagems
the Spirit convicted and ravaged him,
he felt himself cursed and condemned,
his blood in the dark superstitiously rushing
toward its own fated end.

When now his mouth did prophesy
it only was to give more time

flüchten könne. So war dieses zweite
Mal. Doch einst: er hatte prophezeit

fast als Kind, als ob ihm jede Ader
mündete in einen Mund aus Erz;
Alle schritten, doch er schritt gerader.
Alle schrieen, doch ihm schrie das Herz.

Und nun war er nichts als dieser Haufen
umgestürzter Würden, Last auf Last;
und sein Mund war wie der Mund der Traufen,
der die Güsse, die zusammenlaufen,
fallen läßt, eh er sie faßt.

Samuels Erscheinung vor Saul

Da schrie die Frau zu Endor auf: Ich sehe —
Der König packte sie am Arme. Wen?
Und da die Starrende beschrieb, noch ehe,
da war ihm schon, er hätte selbst gesehn:

Den, dessen Stimme ihn noch einmal traf:
Was störst du mich? Ich habe Schlaf.
Willst du, weil dir die Himmel fluchen
und weil der Herr sich von dir schloß und schwieg,
in meinem Mund nach einem Siege suchen?
Soll ich dir meine Zähne einzeln sagen?
Ich habe nichts als sie. . . Es schwand. Da schrie
das Weib, die Hände vors Gesicht geschlagen,
als ob sie's sehen müßte: Unterlieg—

Und er, der in der Zeit, die ihm gelang,
das Volk wie ein Feldzeichen überragte,

to him who fled. This time was such.
But once he had prophesied much

when almost still a boy, as if
each vein of his led to a mouth of ore;
all walked but he walked straight and trim.
All called but he from straight within.

And now he'd become nothing but this,
a pile of toppled honor, a chore;
his mouth like the troughs beneath the eaves
made to catch the converging waters of words
did not catch them anymore.

I Samuel 19; Paris, summer 1908

Samuel's Appearance to Saul
(Of the New Poems' Other Part, 1908)

The woman of Endor screamed: I see—
The king seized her arm and said: But whom?
And while she gazed and before she had told
he thought that he himself knew:

there was the one, whose voice pierced once again:
Why interrupt me now? I am asleep.
Do you come searching since the heavens curse
your head and since the Lord withdrew from you
inside my mouth for yet another feat?
Should I spell out each single tooth I have?
It's all I have . . . And then the vision left.
The woman cried, her hands covered her face
as if again she saw his fate: submit—

But he, who in his own good time
had towered above his people like a victory flag,

fiel hin, bevor er noch zu klagen wagte,
so sicher war sein Untergang.

Die aber, die ihn wider Willen schlug,
hoffte, daß er sich faßte und vergäße;
und als sie hörte, daß er nie mehr äße,
ging sie hinaus und schlachtete und buk

und brachte ihn dazu, daß er sich setzte;
er saß wie einer, der zu viel vergißt;
alles was war, bis auf das Eine, Letzte.
Dann aß er wie ein Knecht zu Abend ißt.

Tröstung des Elia

Er hatte das getan und dies, den Bund
wie jenen Altar wider aufzubauen,
zu dem sein weitgeschleudertes Vertrauen
zurück als Feuer fiel von ferne, und
hatte er dann nicht Hunderte zerhauen,
 weil sie ihm stanken mit dem Baal im Mund,

am Bache schlachtend bis ans Abendgrauen,
das mit dem Regengrau sich groß verband.

Doch als ihn von der Königin der Bote
nach solchem Werktag antrat und bedrohte,
da lief er wie ein Irrer in das Land,

so lange bis er unterm Ginsterstrauche
wie weggeworfen aufbrach in Geschrei
das in der Wüste brüllte: Gott, gebrauche
mich länger nicht. Ich bin entzwei.

fell down and did not dare argue:
so certain was his death.

But the one beating him against her will
was hoping he would recover and forget
and when she saw him refusing to eat,
she proceeded to butcher and bake

and had him sit down in the end;
he sat like one who forgets too much:
all the past he forgot but for that;
then ate like a hungry farmhand would.

I Samuel 28; Paris, August 22-September 5, 1907

The Comforting of Elijah
(Of the New Poems' Other Part, 1908)

To patch the pact he had done this and that:
the altar he had been restoring again
on which his far-reaching faith and trust
from a distance could generate flames;
had he not hundreds of people ground up
for the way they reeked of Baal in their mouths

in a watery slaughter till dusk,
whose gray matched that of a rainy day?

Yet when a soldier the queen had sent
approached after he had done things like that,
he ran off and acted like mad

and ran through the land till he by a shrub
of juniper broke into screams that sent
the desert their echoes: O God, do not
employ me this way. I am spent.

Doch grade da kam ihn der Engel ätzen
mit einer Speise, die er tief empfing,
so daß er lange dann an Weideplätzen
und Wassern immer zum Gebirge ging,

zu dem der Herr um seinetwillen kam:
Im Sturme nicht und nicht im Sich-Zerspalten
der Erde, der entlang in schweren Falten
ein leeres Feuer ging, fast wie aus Scham
über des Ungeheuren ausgeruhtes
Hinstürzen zu dem angekommnen Alten,
der ihn im sanften Sausen seines Blutes
erschreckt und zugedeckt vernahm.

Esther

Die Dienerinnen kämmten sieben Tage
die Asche ihres Grams und ihrer Plage
Neige und Niederschlag aus ihrem Haar,
und trugen es und sonnten es im Freien
und speisten es mit reinen Spezereien
noch diesen Tag und den: dann aber war

die Zeit gekommen, da sie, ungeboten,
zu keiner Frist, wie eine von den Toten
den drohend offenen Palast betrat,
um gleich, gelegt auf ihre Kammerfrauen,

But just right then the angel appeared
with food of which he could take his fill,
so that for some time he proceeded to walk
to the waters and fields up the hills,

where for his sake the Lord had gone.
Not in a storm or the splitting earth
or its rims along which burn eternal flames,
but almost out of embarrassment
by the way the Lord Almighty had been
poised while hurrying toward him
that he heard, half afraid and covered up,
God's voice in the rush of his blood.

*I Kings 19; Elijah had fought against the Baal cult introduced by
King Ahab, whose wife, Jezebel, is believed to have brought the cult
from Tyros and persecuted the Israelite prophets. After Elijah had fled
from Jezebel to Mount Horeb, where Moses had received the Ten
Commandments, God appears to him not in a whirlwind or earth-
quake or fire, but in a still small voice. Paris, early summer 1908*

Esther
(Of the New Poems' Other Part, 1908)

Her servants combed for seven days
the ashes of her grief and of her pain
and all its residue out of her hair,
and carried it and aired it in the sun
and nourished it with purest essences
this day, and yet another one:

but then, the time at last had come for her,
uninvited, undeterred, like someone dead
to step through the ominously open doors
of the palace while leaning against her maids,

am Ende ihres Weges Den zu schauen,
an dem man stirbt, wenn man ihm naht.

Er glänzte so, daß sie die Kronrubine
aufflammen fühlte, die sie an sich trug;
sie füllte sich ganz rasch mit seiner Miene
wie ein Gefäß und war schon voll genug

und floß schon über von des Königs Macht,
bevor sie noch den dritten Saal durchschritt,
der sie mit seiner Wände Malachit
grün überlief. Sie hatte nicht gedacht,

so langen Gang zu tun mit allen Steinen,
die schwerer wurden von des Königs Scheinen
und kalt von ihrer Angst. Sie ging und ging—

Und als sie endlich, fast von nahe, ihn,
aufruhend auf dem Thron von Turmalin,
sich türmen sah, so wirklich wie ein Ding:

empfing die rechte von den Dienerinnen
die Schwindende und hielt sie zu dem Sitze.
Er rührte sie mit seines Szepters Spitze:
. . . und sie begriff es ohne Sinne, innen.

to glimpse at the end of her walk the one
of whom one dies when going near.

He shimmered so that she could sense
the crown jewel she wore alighting on her;
and it filled itself quickly with his countenance
like a vessel, and was already filled

and spilled over from the king's might
before the third room was even crossed
which, with its green walls of malachite,
cast a green on her. She had not

thought to be walking with these stones this long
growing heavier from the king's gleam
and cold from her fear. She walked on—

And when she finally, almost there, saw him
resting on the throne of tourmaline
and raising himself, real like a thing:

there received the maid servant on her right
the fainting one and brought her to the seat.
He touched her with his scepter's crown:
. . . she knew, without seeing, within.

*The episode of Esther's approaching the king, her maids accompany-
ing her, and her swooning is taken from the Greek version of the
Book of Esther found in the Apocrypha, which differs significantly
from the Hebrew version found in the Old Testament of Protestant
Bibles. Rilke's poem is a close rendering of the episode recorded in the
Septuagint, the Greek translation of the Old Testament canon. See*

Jeremia

Einmal war ich weich wie früher Weizen,
doch, du Rasender, du hast vermocht,
mir das hingehaltne Herz zu reizen,
daß es jetzt wie eines Löwen kocht.

Welchen Mund hast du mir zugemutet,
damals, da ich fast ein Knabe war:
eine Wunde wurde er: nun blutet
aus ihm Unglücksjahr um Unglücksjahr.

Täglich tönte ich von neuen Nöten,
die du, Unersättlicher, ersannst,
und sie konnten mir den Mund nicht töten;
sieh du zu, wie du ihn stillen kannst,

wenn, die wir zerstoßen und zerstören,
erst verloren sind und fernverlaufen
und vergangen sind in der Gefahr:
denn dann will ich in den Trümmerhaufen
endlich meine Stimme wiederhören,
die von Anfang an ein Heulen war.

Chapter 15:1-16 of Esther with Additions in the Apocrypha. Esther risks her life when unbeckoned she approaches her husband, King Ahasuerus of Persia, who had issued an edict to kill all Jews in the Persian provinces. Her walk to the king's throne, intended to prevent the massacre of her own people, parallels entering the Holy of Holies in the temple of Jerusalem and the danger of coming near God. Having fainted, she still knows the mercy of having been received not through her senses, but from within. The fainting of Esther is a frequent theme of paintings of the Renaissance. Paris, early summer 1908.

Jeremiah
(Of the New Poems' Other Part, 1908)

At one time I was soft like early wheat,
but you, raging one, did succeed
to incite my heart offered up to you,
so it boils like that of wild beasts.

What kind of mouth you imposed on me,
back then, when I was barely grown:
a wound it became: and from it seep
misfortunes, on and on.

Daily I resounded with the latest strains,
which you, the ever hungry, thought up;
since they were unable to kill my mouth,
you, go see to it that it shuts;

as soon as those we sought to crush and destroy
have dissipated and run away
and melted in fear out of sight:
I should like, amidst the debris,
recover my voice that was from the start
a weeping and a cry.

Jeremiah is called the weeping prophet because of the pain over his fruitless efforts to call the people of Judah back from their heathen practices and unto repentance; he is unable to avert the Lord's punishment of Judah, so that its inhabitants are taken into Babylonian captivity following the fall of Jerusalem in B.C. 586. Jeremiah is also credited with the authorship of the Book of Lamentations. Paris, mid-August, 1907.

II. Die Heilige Maria

Geburt Mariae

O was muß es die Engel gekostet haben,
nicht aufzusingen plötzlich, wie man aufweint,
da sie doch wußten: in dieser Nacht wird dem Knaben
die Mutter geboren, dem Einen, der bald erscheint.

Schwingend verschwiegen sie sich und zeigten die Richtung,
wo, allein,, das Gehöft lag des Joachim,
ach, sie fühlten in sich und im Raum die reine Verdichtung,
aber es durfte keiner nieder zu ihm.

Denn die beiden waren schon so außer sich vor Getue.
Eine Nachbarin kam und klugte und wußte nicht wie,
und der Alte, vorsichtig, ging und verhielt das Gemuhe
einer dunkelen Kuh. Denn so war es noch nie.

Die Darstellung Mariae im Tempel

Um zu begreifen, wie sie damals war,
mußt du dich erst an eine Stelle rufen,
wo Säulen in dir wirken; wo du Stufen
nachfühlen kannst; wo Bogen voll Gefahr
den Abgrund eines Raumes überbrücken,
der in dir blieb, weil er aus solchen Stücken
getürmt war, daß du sie nicht mehr aus dir
ausheben kannst: du rissest dich denn ein.
Bist du so weit, ist alles in dir Stein,

II. The Virgin Mary

The Birth of Mary
(The Life of the Virgin Mary, 1912)

How must the angels have struggled
not to erupt in praises, like one might erupt in tears,
the minute they knew that tonight would be born
the mother, who'd soon bear the son.

Wings a-flapping they held their tongues pointing the direction
to where the only house was that of Joachim's;
o, how they could feel in the air the purest complexion,
but none was allowed to stoop down to him.

For the couple were already upset enough.
A neighbor had come to share what she barely knew,
and the old man had silenced a cow that mooed
as a precaution—and all seemed new.

*According to the apocryphal Protevangelium of James, Mary was the
daughter of Joachim and Anne and was born in Jerusalem. The legend
of Mary's birth is frequently depicted in Byzantine art.*

Presentation of Mary in the Temple
(The Life of the Virgin Mary, 1912)

If you want to comprehend the way she was,
first transpose yourself into a place
teeming with pillars and stairs you can climb,
and archways daring to bridge the abyss
of emptiness remaining inside,
outlining what shapes your identity and
what would be most difficult to remove
without tearing gashes in you.
Once you are there, all is stone and wall,

Wand, Aufgang, Durchblick, Wölbung—, so probier
den großen Vorhang, den du vor dir hast,
ein wenig wegzuzerrn mit beiden Händen:
da glänzt es von ganz hohen Gegenständen
und übertrifft dir Atem und Getast.
Hinauf, hinab, Palast steht auf Palast,
Geländer strömen breiter aus Geländern
und tauchen oben auf an solchen Rändern
daß dich, wie du sie siehst, der Schwindel faßt.
Dabei macht ein Gewölk aus Räucherständern
die Nähe trüb; aber das Fernste zielt
in dich hinein mit seinen graden Strahlen—,
und wenn jetzt Schein aus klaren Flammenschalen
auf langsam nahenden Gewändern spielt;
wie hältst du's aus?

Sie aber kam und hob
den Blick, um dieses alles anzuschauen.
(Ein Kind, ein kleines Mädchen zwischen Frauen.)
Dann stieg sie ruhig, voller Selbstvertrauen,
dem Aufwand zu, der sich verwöhnt verschob:
So sehr war alles, was die Menschen bauen,
schon überwogen von dem Lob

in ihrem Herzen. Von der Lust
sich hinzugeben an die innern Zeichen:
Die Eltern meinten, sie hinaufzureichen,
der Drohende mit der Juwelenbrust
empfing sie scheinbar: Doch sie ging durch alle,
klein wie sie war, aus jeder Hand hinaus
und in ihr Los, das, höher als die Halle,
schon fertig war, und schwerer als das Haus.

ascent, vista, and vault—so try
gently pulling the curtain away
in front with both of your hands:
there is a luster of tall and towering things
that take away your breath and elude your touch.
Palace is stacked upon palace, and up
and down run railings, expand, grow wide,
their lines emerging at staggering heights
so your head begins to spin.
Meanwhile, the incense from censers dilutes
proximity; yet what's farthest removed
aims its shimmer directly at you—,
and when the light from the votive lamps
plays off your clothes as you slowly approach,
all seeing is hard to endure.

But she came and simply raised her eyes
and at everything she began to look
(a child, a girl among womenfolk).
And then she moved with self-confidence
toward this prideful magnificence,
showing that human buildings are dwarfed
by devotion in one single heart.

She reveled in the pleasure to surrender
to the stirrings awaking in her.
The parents presumed they did dedicate her
and the Almighty had taken her in:
But she who had merely proceeded from them,
was headed past hands unto Providence,
—more spacious and massive than house or hall,
and built for her ages ago.

Mariae Verkündigung

Nicht daß ein Engel eintrat (das erkenn),
erschreckte sie. Sowenig andre, wenn
ein Sonnenstrahl oder der Mond bei Nacht
in ihrem Zimmer sich zu schaffen macht,
auffahren—, pflegte sie an der Gestalt,
in der ein Engel ging, sich zu entrüsten;
sie ahnte kaum, daß dieser Aufenthalt
mühsam für Engel ist. (O wenn wir wüßten,
wie rein sie war. Hat eine Hirschkuh nicht,
die, liegend, einmal sie im Wald eräugte,
sich so in sie versehn, daß sich in ihr,
ganz ohne Paarigen, das Einhorn zeugte,
das Tier aus Licht, das reine Tier—.)
Nicht, daß er eintrat, aber daß er dicht,
der Engel, eines Jünglings Angesicht
so zu ihr neigte; daß sein Blick und der,
mit dem sie aufsah, so zusammenschlugen
als wäre draußen plötzlich alles leer
und, was Millionen schauten, trieben, trugen,
hineingedrängt in sie: nur sie und er;
Schaun und Geschautes, Aug und Augenweide
sonst nirgends als an dieser Stelle—: sieh,

According to legend, Mary had been dedicated by her parents to God in the Temple of Jerusalem, where she is believed to have taken a vow of perpetual virginity. The spacious opulence of the Temple described here suggests as a visual inspiration of Rilke's the well-known popular etchings of Giovanni Battista Piranesi (1720-78) with their awe-inspiring visions of bafflingly complicated and intimidating architectural spaces with their seeming infinity of massive arches, vaults, piers, and stairways, through which move human figures dwarfed by the immense structures.

Annunciation to Mary
(The Life of the Virgin Mary, 1912)

It was not the angel that entered (this realize)
that frightened her. Just as little as people would be
startled when the sun or the moon
were busying themselves in their room,
that is how little she was stirred
by the angel who had appeared;
though hardly was she aware
that for angels such visits are hard.
(If only we saw how pure she was.
Did not once a doe spotting her in the woods
fall in love with her so much that in her
was conceived, without mating, the unicorn,
the beast of light, the purest one—.)
Not that the angel, with his manly face,
entered but instead bent toward her;
so that his eyes and hers she had raised
collided as if nothing else there was;
and what a million others could see
and push and carried, was compressed
into them: in her and in him;
seeing and what is seen, the eye and the espied,
existed nowhere but between the two of them—:

dieses erschreckt. Und sie erschraken beide.

Dann sang der Engel seine Melodie.

Verkündigung: Die Worte des Engels

Du bist nicht näher an Gott als wir;
wir sind ihm alle weit.
Aber wunderbar sind dir
die Hände benedeit.
So reifen sie bei keiner Frau,
so schimmernd aus dem Saum:
ich bin der Tag, ich bin der Tau,
du aber bist der Baum.

Ich bin jetzt matt, mein Weg war weit,
vergieb mir, ich vergaß,
was Er, der groß in Goldgeschmeid
wie in der Sonne saß,
dir künden ließ, du Sinnende,
(verwirrt hat mich der Raum).
Sieh: ich bin das Beginnende,
du aber bist der Baum.

Ich spanne meine Schwingen aus
und wurde seltsam weit;
jetzt überfließt dein kleines Haus
von meinem großen Kleid.
Und dennoch bist du so allein
wie nie und schaust mich kaum;
das macht: ich bin ein Hauch im Hain,
du aber bist der Baum.

that is what frightens. And they both were.

And only then the angel sang.

Luke 1:26-38

Annunciation: The Words of the Angel
(The Book of Images, 1902/06)

You are no closer to God than any of us;
we all live far and wide.
But it's wonderful how your hands
have been sanctified.
They don't find a match in other women's,
so brilliant from beneath their sleeves:
I am the day, I am the dew,
but you are tree.

I am rather tired now, my journey was long,
forgive that I forgot
that he, who sat in gilded garb
like in a ray of light,
sends news to you, you quiet one
(this room here startled me).
Look: I am the beginning one,
but you are tree.

I spread my wings apart
and became oddly broad;
now your little house is flooded
with my coat.
And still, you are so all alone
as never before, me you hardly see;
because I am just breath in woods,
but you are tree.

Die Engel alle bange so,
lassen einander los:
noch nie war das Verlangen so,
so ungewiß und groß.
Vielleicht, daß etwas bald geschieht,
das du im Traum begreifst.
Gegrüßt sei, meine Seele sieht:
du bist bereit und reifst.
Du bist ein großes, hohes Tor,
und aufgehn wirst du bald.
Du, meines Liedes liebstes Ohr,
jetzt fühle ich: mein Wort verlor
sich in dir wie im Wald.

So kam ich und vollendete
dir tausendeinen Traum.
Gott sah mich an; er blendete. . .

Du aber bist der Baum.

Magnificat

Sie kam den Hang herauf, schon schwer, fast ohne
an Trost zu glauben, Hoffnung oder Rat;
doch da die hohe tragende Matrone
ihr ernst und stolz entgegentrat

und alles wußte ohne ihr Vertrauen,
da war sie plötzlich an ihr ausgeruht;
vorsichtig hielten sich die vollen Frauen,
bis daß die junge sprach: Mir ist zumut,

All the angels are worried now,
letting go of each other's hands:
never before was there such a longing,
so uncertain and immense.
Perhaps it will come about soon
and you will grasp it as if in a dream.
Blessings to you, my soul perceives
you are ready and ripe to receive.
You are a great and lofty gate
and about to open up.
You are my song's most beloved ear.
I feel there disappears and seeps
into you my word.

That's how I came and completed
your dream among a thousand and one.
And with blinding eyes God looked at me . . . .

But you are tree.

Luke 1:26-38; Berlin-Schmargendorf, July 1899

Magnificat
(Of the New Poems' Other Part, 1908)

She climbed up the hill, heavy with child,
nearly without hope for solace or succor;
but when the other, also pregnant, met her
so solemn and bold

and knew everything without having been told,
she could at last repose and rest;
carefully the two women embraced
until the younger one said: It seems,

als war ich, Liebe, von nun an für immer.
Gott schüttet in der Reichen Eitelkeit
fast ohne hinzusehen ihren Schimmer;
doch sorgsam sucht er sich ein Frauenzimmer
und füllt sie an mit seiner fernsten Zeit.

Daß er mich fand. Bedenk nur; und Befehle
um meinetwillen gab von Stern zu Stern—.

Verherrliche und hebe, meine Seele,
so hoch du kannst: den Herrn.

Mariae Heimsuchung

Noch erging sie's leicht im Anbeginne,
doch im Steigen manchmal ward sie schon
ihres wunderbaren Leibes inne,—
und dann stand sie, atmend, auf den hohn

Judenbergen. Aber nicht das Land,
ihre Fülle war um sie gebreitet;
gehend fühlte sie: man überschreitet
nie die Größe, die sie jetzt empfand.

Und es drängte sie, die Hand zu legen
auf den andern Leib, der weiter war.
Und die Frauen schwankten sich entgegen
und berührten sich Gewand und Haar.

Jede, voll von ihrem Heiligtume,
schützte sich mit der Gevatterin.

my dearest, I might live on for good.
God pours haphazardly into the wealthy one
vanity without barely looking;
but he is careful and choosey when pouring
and filling another with eternal charm.

Just think that he found me and ordered
the stars around on account of me—

So, magnify and raise, my soul,
as high as you manage: the Lord.

Luke 1:39-56

Visitation
(The Life of the Virgin Mary, 1912)

It was still easy for her in the beginning,
only when climbing she would
be aware of her heavy womb,—
and then she stood, breathing,

on the Jewish mountains. But not the land
spread about her, but her fullness; and
while walking she knew: nowhere
was there such fullness as hers.

And she felt compelled to feel with her hand
the womb of hers who was further along.
Toward each other they swayingly stepped
and caressed the dress and the hair.

Each woman was filled with sacred life
and safe and at ease with the relative.

Ach der Heiland in ihr war noch Blume,
doch den Täufer in dem Schooß der Muhme
riß die Freude schon zum Hüpfen hin.

Argwohn Josephs

Und der Engel sprach und gab sich Müh
an dem Mann, der seine Fäuste ballte:
Aber siehst du nicht an jeder Falte,
daß sie kühl ist wie die Gottesfrüh.

Doch der andre sah ihn finster an,
murmelnd nur: Was hat sie so verwandelt?
Doch da schrie der Engel: Zimmermann,
merkst du's noch nicht, daß der Herrgott handelt?

Weil du Bretter machst, in deinem Stolze,
willst du wirklich den zu Rede stelln,
der bescheiden aus dem gleichen Holze
Blätter treiben macht und Knospen schwelln?

Er begriff. Und wie er jetzt die Blicke,
recht erschrocken, zu dem Engel hob,
war der fort. Da schob er seine dicke
Mütze langsam ab. Dann sang er lob.

And though the savior was hardly in bloom,
the Baptist in the cousin's womb
already jumped for joy.

*Luke 1:39-45; in contrast to the biblical account, Rilke has the two
women touch each other, which is a common way of depicting the
Visitation in Byzantine art.*

Joseph's Suspicion
(The Life of the Virgin Mary, 1912)

And the angel did all it could when talking
with the man whose fists were clenched:
Don't you see in her facial expression
she is untouched by passion, undrenched?

But the man only scowled and mumbled:
What is it that has this brought on?
And the angel cried out: O carpenter,
don't you see what the good Lord has done?

Because you take pride in your boards and beams
do you really want to confront and quiz
him who modestly from the same wood
makes the buds erupt and the leaves.

He understood and raised his head
fairly frightened toward the angel above;
but the angel had left. And so he took
off his cap. And then he praised God.

*Matthew 1:18-25; the biblical account downplays Joseph's suspicion
and rage over the pregnancy of Mary to whom he had been betrothed.*

Rast auf der Flucht in Aegypten

Diese, die noch eben atemlos
flohen mitten aus dem Kindermorden:
o wie waren sie unmerklich groß
über ihrer Wanderschaft geworden.

Kaum noch daß im scheuen Rückwärtsschauen
ihres Schreckens Not zergangen war,
und schon brachten sie auf ihrem grauen
Maultier ganze Städte in Gefahr;

denn so wie sie, klein im großen Land,
—fast ein Nichts—den starken Tempeln nahten,
platzten alle Götzen wie verraten
und verloren völlig den Verstand.

Ist es denkbar, daß von ihrem Gange
alles so verzweifelt sich erbost?
und sie wurden vor sich selber bange,
nur das Kind war namelos getrost.

Immerhin, sie mußten sich darüber
eine Weile setzen. Doch da ging—
sieh: der Baum, der still sie überhing,
wie ein Dienender zu ihnen über:

er verneigte sich. Derselbe Baum,
dessen Kränze toten Pharaonen
für das Ewige die Stirnen schonen,
neigte sich. Er fühlte neue Kronen
blühen. Und sie saßen wie im Traum.

Stop on their Flight to Egypt
(The Life of the Virgin Mary, 1912)

Those who were out of breath
were fleeing the children's murder and deaths;
o how they had matured invisibly
by their pilgrimage.

Hardly had they recovered from this terror
while barely looking back,
that they were on their mule carrying
to new cities the same threat;

for as they were approaching the temples' gates,
as nobodies in this vast land,
all idols split open as if betrayed
and lost their head.

Is it that their walk provoked
in everything rage and alarm?
And they grew rather weary of themselves,
while the child stayed unspeakably calm.

Nonetheless, they had to sit down
for a while. But there came—see:
the tree to lean over them
as in humility:

and then bowed low. The same tree
whose branches, once bent into wreaths,
had preserved for the eternal one the pharaohs.
Now, the tree could feel new growth.
And dreamlike they sat underneath.

Von der Hochzeit zu Kana

Konnte sie denn anders, als auf ihn
stolz sein, der ihr Schlichtestes verschönte?
War nicht selbst die hohe, großgewöhnte
Nacht wie außer sich, da er erschien?

Ging nicht auch, daß er sich einst verloren,
 unerhört zu seiner Glorie aus?
Hatten nicht die Weisesten die Ohren
mit dem Mund vertauscht? Und war das Haus

nicht wie neu von seiner Stimme? Ach
sicher hatte sie zu hundert Malen
ihre Freude an ihm auszustrahlen
sich verwehrt. Sie ging ihm staundend nach.

Aber da bei jenem Hochzeitsfeste,
als es unversehns an Wein gebrach,—
sah sie hin und bat um eine Geste
und begriff nicht, daß er widersprach.

Und dann tat er's. Sie verstand es später,
wie sie ihn in seinen Weg gedrängt:
denn jetzt war er wirklich Wundertäter,
und das ganze Opfer war verhängt,

unaufhaltsam. Ja, es stand geschrieben.
Aber war es damals schon bereit?
Sie: sie hatte es herbeigetrieben
in der Blindheit ihrer Eitelkeit.

Matthew 2:13-15; legend has the couple stop at a city in Egypt, called Heliopolis, where at the sight of the child the idols topple over and shatter into pieces.

Wedding at Cana
(The Life of the Virgin Mary, 1912)

Could she have helped being proud of him,
he who embellished her very modesty?
Was not even the noble and extravagant night
quite beside herself when he appeared?

Did the night not extend herself for his sake,
who looked so lost at first?
Did not even the wisest exchange their ears
for a mouth? And was the house

not like new because of his voice? Certainly,
she had refused a hundred times
to demonstrate plainly her delight in him.
Instead, in awe she followed him around.

But at this wedding feast,
when accidentally the wine ran out,
she looked and requested a sign from him
and couldn't understand when he frowned.

And then he concurred. She understood later
how she had forced him unto his path:
for now he was already miracle worker,
and soon would be victim of wrath

inescapably. Yes, it had been prophesied.
But had it been meant this soon?
Had she not precipitated his death
through the blindness of her pride?

An dem Tisch voll Früchten und Gemüsen
freute sie sich mit und sah nicht ein,
daß das Wasser ihrer Tränendrüsen
Blut geworden war mit diesem Wein.

Vor der Passion

O hast du dies gewollt, du hättest nicht
durch eines Weibes Leib entspringen dürfen:
Heilande muß man in den Bergen schürfen,
wo man das Harte aus dem Harten bricht.

Tut dirs nicht selber leid, dein liebes Tal
so zu verwüsten? Siehe meine Schwäche;
ich habe nichts als Milch- und Tränenbäche,
und du warst immer in der Überzahl.

Mit solchem Aufwand wardst du mir verheißen.
Was tratst du nicht gleich wild aus mir hinaus?
Wenn du nur Tiger brauchst, dich zu zerreißen,
warum erzog man mich im Frauenhaus,

ein weiches reines Kleid für dich zu weben,
darin nicht einmal die geringste Spur
von Naht dich drückt—: so war mein ganzes Leben,
und jetzt verkehrst du plötzlich die Natur.

At the table filled with fruit and legumes
she rejoiced and could not yet find
that the water of her future tears
had turned to blood with this wine.

John 2:1-11

Anticipating the Passion
(The Life of the Virgin Mary, 1912)

If you had really wanted to be strong,
you would not have come from a woman's womb.
For messiahs are quarried from mountains
where the sturdy and strong comes from stone.

Are you not sorry to have despoiled your land
by such limitations? I am weak, don't you see;
I only had streams of milk or tears to offer,
and you were ever so much more than me.

So much ado when your birth to me was announced.
You could have been born fierce and wild from the start.
If you only needed tigers to tear you to pieces,
why did I learn gentleness as an art

by which I wove for you a soft, pure gown
without even the slightest seam
for comfort—: that's how my life has been,
which you now have turned upside down.

Pietà

Jetzt wird mein Elend voll, und namenlos
erfüllt es mich. Ich starre wie des Steins
Inneres starrt.
Hart wie ich bin, weiß ich nur Eins:
Du wurdest groß—
. . . . . . und wurdest groß,
um als zu großer Schmerz
ganz über meines Herzens Fassung
hinauszustehn.
Jetzt liegst du quer durch meinen Schooß,
jetzt kann ich dich nicht mehr
gebären.

Stillung Mariae mit dem Auferstandenen

Was sie damals empfanden: ist es nicht
vor allen Geheimnissen süß
und immer noch irdisch:
da er, ein wenig blaß noch vom Grab,
erleichtert zu ihr trat:
an allen Stellen erstanden.
O zu ihr zuerst. Wie waren sie da
unaussprechlich in Heilung.
Ja sie heilten, das war's. Sie hatten nicht nötig,
sich stark zu berühren.
Er legte ihr eine Sekunde
kaum seine nächstens

Pietà
(The Life of the Virgin Mary, 1912)

My pain has been perfected and fills me up.
I stare like the center
of a slab of rock.
Hard as I am, I know only this:
You became great—
. . . and you became great,
and then you burst the rims of my heart
as a smarting too stark.
Now you lie sideways across my lap;
no longer can I give to you
birth.

*Possibly inspired by Matthias Grünewald's Isenheim Altarpiece,
Sandro Botticelli's "Lamentation over Christ," Michelangelo's
"Pietá," and Rodin's sculpture "Christ and Magdalena"; in 1906,
Rilke had composed another "Pietá" poem as part of the New Poems,
which depicted Jesus' body in Mary Magdalene's arms.*

Mary's Comfort with the Risen One
(The Life of the Virgin Mary, 1912)

What they experienced then: is it not
above all mysteries and sweet
and still of this earth:
that he, a little pale yet from the grave,
could approach her with relief:
having been fully raised.
Yes, to her first. How they were
in healing immersed. Yes,
they were being healed, that was it.
They did not need to strongly touch.
He placed but for a second
his soon-to-be eternal hand

ewige Hand an die frauliche Schulter.
Und sie begannen
still wie die Bäume im Frühling,
unendlich zugleich,
diese Jahreszeit
ihres äußersten Umgangs.

Vom Tode Mariae
(Drei Stücke)

I.

Derselbe große Engel, welcher einst
ihr der Gebärdung Botschaft niederbrachte,
stand da, abwartend daß sie ihn beachte,
und sprach: Jetzt wird es Zeit, daß du erscheinst.
Und sie erschrak wie damals und erwies
sich wider als die Magd, ihn tief bejahend.
Er aber strahlte und, unendlich nahend,
schwand er wie in ihr Angesicht—und hieß
die weithin ausgegangenen Bekehrer
zusammenkommen in das Haus am Hang,
das Haus des Abendmahls. Sie kamen schwerer
und traten bange ein: Da lag, entlang
die schmale Bettstatt, die in Untergang
und Auserwählung rätselhaft Getauchte,
ganz unversehrt, wie eine Ungebrauchte,
und achtete auf englischen Gesang.
Nun da sie all hinter ihren Kerzen
abwarten sah, riß sie vom Übermaß
der Stimmen sich und schenkte noch von Herzen
die beiden Kleider fort, die sie besaß,
und hob ihr Antlitz auf zu dem und dem. . .
(O Ursprung nameloser Tränen-Bäche).

on her womanly shoulder, and then
they commenced,
quiet like trees in spring,
both at once for all eternity
the season of their extraordinary
connection.

Death of Mary
(The Life of the Virgin Mary, 1912)

I.

The same big angel who once had laid
before her the message of the birth,
stood waiting for her to look up and said:
It is now time for you to appear.
And afraid as before she became
the handmaiden, saying yes again.
But he beamed and, infinitely close,
disappeared behind her face—and called
the disciples far away at work
to gather in the house on the hill, the one
of the last meal. And they came so grave
and entered with heavy hearts: There she lay
on the small bed, she who had been
miraculously chosen and steeped
into humility unharmed, untouched,
and was listening to angelic song.
Since she saw them waiting behind
their candle light, she tore herself away
from the abundance of song, then gave
away the last two dresses she owned
and kindly lifted her face to this one and that . . .
(Source of tear-filled rivulets).

Sie aber legte sich in ihre Schwäche
und zog die Himmel an Jerusalem
so nah heran, daß ihre Seele nur,
austretend, sich ein wenig strecken mußte:
schon hob er sie, der alles von ihr wußte,
hinein in ihre göttliche Natur.

II.

Wer hat bedacht, daß bis zu ihrem Kommen
der viele Himmel unvollständig war?
Der Auferstandne hatte Platz genommen,
doch neben ihm, durch vierundzwanzig Jahr,
war leer der Sitz. Und sie begannen schon
sich an die reine Lücke zu gewöhnen,
die wie verheilt war, denn mit seinem schönen
Hinüberscheinen füllte sie der Sohn.

So auch sie, die in die Himmel trat,
nicht auf ihn zu, so sehr es sie verlangte;
dort war kein Platz, nur Er war dort und prangte
mit einer Strahlung, die ihr wehe tat.
Doch da sie jetzt, die rührende Gestalt,
sich zu den neuen Seligen gesellte
und unauffällig, licht zu licht, sich stellte,
da brach aus ihrem Sein ein Hinterhalt
von solchem Glanz, daß der von ihr erhellte
Engel geblendet aufschrie: Wer ist die?
Ein Staunen war. Dann sahn sie alle, wie
Gott-Vater oben unsern Herrn verhielt,
so daß, von milder Dämmerung umspielt,
die leere Stille wie ein wenig Leid
sich zeigte, eine Spur von Einsamkeit,
wie etwas, was er noch ertrug, ein Rest
irdischer Zeit, ein trockenes Gebrest—.

Into her feeble state she leaned,
drawing the heavens unto Jerusalem
so close that her soul only needed
to stretch somewhat:
the one who knew her in full, had placed
her already in the heavenly estate.

II.

Who would have thought that until her coming
the entire heavens were incomplete?
The risen one had taken a seat,
but next to him, for twenty-four years,
the seat had been empty. And they had begun
to get used to the vacancy,
which seemed to have closed up and healed;
the son with his radiant gleaming had it filled.

Thus, not even she who stepped into heaven
walked toward him, despite his pleas;
there was no room, only he was there
with a radiance that stung with its gleam.
But when she, the gentle figure,
sought to blend with other newcomers there
and sidled with them inconspicuously,
there broke from her such sheen
of such a might, that the angel next to her
blinded by it, cried: Who is she?
There was surprise. Then they saw
how the Father in heaven implored our Lord,
so that caressed by a mild dawn
the empty spot emerged like a small wound,
like a trace of loneliness,
like something he still endured,
a residue of earthly time, a dry compress—.

Man sah nach ihr; sie schaute ängstlich hin,
weit vorgeneigt, als fühlte sie: ich bin
sein längster Schmerz—: und stürzte plötzlich vor.
Die Engel aber nahmen sie zu sich
und stützten sie und sangen seliglich
und trugen sie das letzte Stück empor.

III.

Doch vor dem Apostel Thomas, der
kam, da es zu spät war, trat der schnelle
längst darauf gefaßte Engel her
und befahl an der Begräbnisstelle:

Dräng den Stein beiseite. Willst du wissen,
wo die ist, die dir das Herz bewegt:
Sieh: sie ward wie ein Lavendelkissen
eine Weile da hineingelegt,

daß die Erde künftig nach ihr rieche
in den Falten wie ein feines Tuch.
Alles Tote (fühlst du), alles Sieche
ist betäubt von ihrem Wohl-Geruch.

Schau den Leinwand: wo ist eine Bleiche,
wo er blendend wird und geht nicht ein?
Dieses Licht aus dieser reinen Leiche
war ihm klärender als Sonnenschein.

Staunst du nicht, wie sanft sie ihm entging?
Fast als wär sie's noch, nichts ist verschoben.
Doch die Himmel sind erschüttert oben:
Mann, knie hin und sieh mir nach und sing.

And they looked at her; and she, afraid,
leaned forward as if to say: I am
his most enduring pain—: and fell suddenly
forward. But the angels caught her and braced
her fall and happily, for the final stretch,
carried her in.

III.

But on earth the apostle Thomas, who had been late,
was approached quickly by an angel
who had been well prepared for it
and ordered him at the tomb:

Push the stone away. Do you want to know
where she is who has touched your heart:
Look: she was like a lavender pillow
placed in here just for a little while,

so the earth would smell like her
in its folds like a precious sheet.
Everything dead (smell it), everything sick
is numbed by her aroma so sweet.

Look at the linen cloth: where is it pale,
where bright and where did it shrink?
This light from her pure body
bleached it better than sun and wind.

Are you not surprised at how gently she left?
As if she was still here, nothing askew.
But the heavens have been shaking above:
So, kneel and sing and look where I'll go!

Himmelfahrt Mariae

I.

Köstliche, o Öl, das oben will,
blauer Rauchrand aus dem Räucherkorbe,
grad-hinan vertönende Theorbe,
Milch des Irdischen, entquill,

still die Himmel, die noch klein sind, nähre
das dir anruht, das verweinte Reich:
Goldgewordne wie die hohe Ähre,
Reingewordne wie das Bild im Teich.

Wie wir nächtens, daß die Brunnen gehen,
hören im vereinsamten Gehör:
bist du, Steigende, in unserm Sehen
ganz allein. Wie in ein Nadelöhr

will mein langer Blick in dir sich fassen,
eh du diesem Sichtlichen entfliehst,—
daß du ihn, wenn auch ganz weiß gelassen,
durch die farbenechten Himmel ziehst.

The poem moves through three stages in the life of the Virgin Mary: her last days on earth and her dormition, or "falling asleep," in the company of the disciples; her coronation in heaven by Jesus upon God's beckoning; and her venerated status on earth among Christ's followers. The coronation of Mary became a standard part of the iconography of Mary during the twelfth century, regularly depicting her as sitting at Christ's right hand; it was a continuation of this understanding when later painters showed Christ or God the Father or the entire Trinity investing her with the crown. The dormition, or koimesis, of the Virgin Mary depicts her soul as being taken up to heaven; its icon is central in Eastern churches.

Assumption of Mary
(Poems 1906-1926)

I.

Precious one, you who are oil longing to float,
blue smoke from the censer's cup,
steadily resounding stringed instrument,
earthly milk, rise up

and nurture the heavens still in their infancy,
feed the tear-filled kingdom entrusted to you,
you who became golden like the grain's ear,
you who became pure like the face of the sea.

The same way our solitary ear at night
can discern the well waters run, you are,
rising one, in our eyes the only one.
Like at the eye of a needle, my gaze

aims at you wishing to comprehend myself
until you vanish from sight—
and then you draw my eyes, left blank,
through the colorfast skies.

II.

Nicht nur aus dem Schaun der Jünger, welchen
deines Kleides leichte Wehmut bleibt:
ach, du nimmst dich aus den Blumenkelchen,
aus dem Vogel, der den Flug beschreibt;

aus dem vollen Offensein der Kinder,
aus dem Euter und dem Kaun der Kuh—;
alles wird um eine Milde minder,
nur die Himmel innen nehmen zu.

Hingerissne Frucht aus unserm Grunde,
Beere, die du voller Süße stehst,
laß uns fühlen, wie du in dem Munde
der entzückten Seligkeit zergehst.

Denn wir bleiben, wo du fortkamst. Jede
Stelle unten will getröstet sein.
Neig uns Gnade, stärk uns wie mit Wein.
Denn vom Einsehn ist da nicht die Rede.

II.

You not only remove yourself from the gaze
of the disciples you left behind:
you also remove yourself from the flower cups,
from the bird marking its flight;

from the utter openness of the children,
from the udder and the chewing of the cow—:
everything loses a little of its softness,
only the heavens grow.

You are fruit snatched out of our life,
a berry hanging round and sweet;
simply let us taste how you melt
on the tongue of eternity.

For we remain blind down here where you left us.
And each place here desires solace and peace.
Grant us at least grace and courage,
since seeing down here has ceased.

*According to apocryphal legend and church tradition, Mary died at
Ephesus, or at Jerusalem, in 48. Rilke says she died twenty-four years
after Jesus' death on the cross. The belief that her body was assumed
into heaven is among the oldest traditions of the Church, and its feast
day has been celebrated since the sixth century on August 15. It was
declared dogma by Pope Pius XII in 1950. Ronda, January 1913.*

III. Jesus Christus

Verkündigung über den Hirten

Seht auf, ihre Männer. Männer dort am Feuer,
die ihr den grenzenlosen Himmel kennt,
Sterndeuter, hierher! Seht, ich bin ein neuer
steigender Stern. Mein ganzes Wesen brennt
und strahlt so stark und ist so ungeheuer
voll Licht, daß mir das tiefe Firmament
nicht mehr genügt. Laßt meinen Glanz hinein
in euer Dasein: Oh, die dunklen Blicke,
die dunklen Herzen, nächtige Geschicke
die euch erfüllen. Hirten, wie allein
bin ich in euch. Auf einmal wird mir Raum.
Staunet ihr nicht: der große Brotfruchtbaum
warf einen Schatten. Ja, das kam von mir.
Ihr Unerschrockenen, o wüßtet ihr,
wie jetzt auf eurem schauenden Gesichte
die Zukunft scheint. In diesem starken Lichte
wird viel geschehen. Euch vertau ichs, denn
ihr seid verschwiegen; euch Gradgläubigen
redet hier alles. Glut und Regen spricht,
der Vögel Zug, der Wind und was ihr seid,
keins überwiegt und wächst zur Eitelkeit
sich mästend an. Ihr haltet nicht
die Dinge auf im Zwischenraum der Brust
um sie zu quälen. So wie seine Lust
durch einen Engel strömt, so treibt durch euch
das Irdische. Und wenn ein Dorngesträuch
aufflammte plötzlich, dürfte noch aus ihm
der Ewige euch rufen, Cherubim,
wenn sie geruhten neben eurer Herde
einherzuschreiten, wunderten euch nicht:

III. Jesus Christ

Annunciation to the Shepherds
(The Life of the Virgin Mary, 1912)

Get up, you men over there by the fire,
you who know so well the infinite sky,
stargazers, over here! Look, I am new.
My entire being is erupting as star
into light so strong and brilliant,
for which the firmament has become too small.
Allow my glow into your life:
Oh, these dark eyes, the hearts pitch black,
the nightly stories that run through you deep.
Shepherds, I enjoy being alone in you.
All at once I have room.
Don't be surprised at the great mulberry tree
casting a shadow. Well, it was mine.
You undaunted ones, if only you knew
that on your gazing faces appears
the future. In this strong light much
will happen. To you I entrust this light
for you can keep it quiet; to you of plain piety
everything is revealed. Amber and rain speak,
the birds' migration, the wind and what you are,
nothing reigns above the other
or reaches for rank with pride.
You do not mitigate the flow of things
in the interval, so as to torture them.
Just like joy runs through an angel,
the earth's delights are running through you.
And when a thornbush bursts into flames,
the Eternal One could still call on you,
and the cherubim beside your herds
would leave you nonplused:

ihr stürztet euch auf euer Angesicht,
betetet an und nenntet dies die Erde.

Doch dieses war. Nun soll ein Neues sein,
von dem der Erdkreis ringender sich weitet.
Was ist ein Dörnicht uns: Gott fühlt sich ein
in einer Jungfrau Schooß. Ich bin der Schein
von ihrer Innigkeit, der euch geleitet.

Geburt Christi

Hättest du der Einfalt nicht, wie sollte
dir geschehn, was jetzt die Nacht erhellt?
Sieh, der Gott, der über Völkern grollte,
macht sich mild und kommt in dir zur Welt.

Hast du dir ihn größer vorgestellt?

Was ist Größe? Quer durch alle Maße,
die er durchstreicht, geht sein grades Los.
Selbst ein Stern hat keine solche Straße.
Siehst du, diese Könige sind groß,

und sie schleppen dir vor deinen Schooß

Schätze, die sie für die größten halten,
und du staunst vielleicht bei dieser Gift—:
aber schau in deines Tuches Falten,
wie er jetzt schon alles übertrifft.

Aller Amber, den man weit verschifft,

you would only fall on your face
and worship and call it the earth.

But this is gone. A new thing has come,
whereby this earth expands its glory in melodies.
What is a thornbush when God slowly seeps
into the womb of a virgin? I am the ray
of her being that's been pointing your way.

Luke 2:8-20

The Birth of Christ
(The Life of the Virgin Mary, 1912)

If it weren't for simple-mindedness,
how else could you have grasped
that the God who raged over the nations
has turned mild now and is born in us?

Did you imagine him thus?

What is greatness? Beyond all measure
he reaches through it and straight across.
Even a star has no such far-reaching orbits.
And then look at these mighty lords,

carrying and placing in your lap

treasures they consider precious and great,
and perhaps you are amazed at them—:
but one look at your swaddling cloth
already outshines

all the amber that is traded in the world,

jeder Goldschmuck und das Luftgewürze,
das sich trübend in die Sinne streut:
alles dieses war von rascher Kürze,
und am Ende hat man es bereut.

Aber (du wirst sehen): Er erfreut.

Die Kinder

Das war
ein Mann inmitten einer Kinderschar.
Schlicht um die Schultern lag ihm der Talar,
und heimathell war ihm das Heilandshaar.
Und wie um einen frühen Frühlingstag
sich, jäherwacht, die Blüten staunend scharen,
so kamen Kinder zu dem Wunderbaren,
den keiner von den Alten nennen mag.
Die Kinder aber kennen ihn schon lang
und drängen in das offne Tor der Arme—
ein blasses betet: Du bist das "Erbarme,"
nach dem die Mutter ihre Hände rang.
Und leise flüstert ihm das wangenwarme:
"Nichtwahr, du wohnst im Sonnenuntergang,
dort wo die Berge groß und golden sind.
Dir winkt der Wipfel und dir singt der Wind,
und guten Kindern kommst du in die Träume."
Da neigen alle sich wie Birkenbäume.
Es neigen sich die Blonden und die Braunen

every gold ring and the scented air
barely satisfies and only teases:
these are of such brief delight
and one wonders why one cares.

But (you'll see): He pleases.

The poem is based on the legend of the wise men (Matthew 2:1-11)
and may have been written during the Worpswede years, inspired by
Heinrich Vogeler's paintings. Vogeler's illustration made for this poem
in 1912, though never published in conjunction with it, was titled Die
Heiligen Drei Könige (The Three Holy Kings).

Christ and the Children
(Christ—Eleven Visions, 1896/98)

There he once was,
a man amidst a children's crowd.
The cape hung about him modestly
and fair was the savior's hair.
And like the flowers that shoot up galore
on early days in spring,
the children flock to him,
while adults rarely mention his name.
For children have been friends with him for long
and they hurry to the gate of his embrace.
A pale one says, "You surely are the grace
for which my mother daily lifts her hands."
Another whispers cheek-to-cheek:
"It's in sunsets that you live, I know,
where the mountains rise up and gleam.
You are waved at by trees and the woods bring you songs,
and good children you meet in their dreams."
And then, like birches, they all bend low.
At his smile both blond and brunette bow,

vor seinem Lächeln, und die Alten staunen.
Und Kinder flüchten sich von allen Seiten
in seinen Segen heim wie in ein Haus,
und lauschen alle. Seine Worte breiten
weit über sie die weißen Flügel aus:

"Hat einmal eins von euch schon nachgedacht,
wie eilig euch die leisen Stunden führen
an jedem Tage und in jeder Nacht
durch tausend Tore und durch tausend Türen.
Noch gehn die Angeln alle leicht und leise
und alle Pforten fallen scheu ins Schloß;
noch bin ich Warner euch und Weggenoß,
doch weit aus meinen Reichen reift die Reise.
Ihr wollt ins Leben, und das bin ich nicht,
ihr müßt ins Dunkel, und ich bin das Licht,
ihr hofft die Freude, ich bin der Verzicht,
ihr sehnt das Glück und—ich bin das Gericht."
Er schwieg. Von ferne horchten auch die Großen.
Dann seufzte er: "Ihr müßt mich nicht verstoßen,
wenn wir zusammen an den Marken stehn.
Mich mitzunehmen seid ihr dann zu jung;
doch schaut ihr mal zurück von euren Fahrten
vielleicht in einen armen Blumengarten,
vielleicht ins Mutterlächeln einer zarten
versehnten Frau, vielleicht in ein Erwarten:
Ich bin die Kindheit, die Erinnerung.
Gebt mir die Hand, schenkt mir [im] Weitergehn
noch einen Blick, der schon ins Leben tauchte,
aus dem der neue und noch niegebrauchte
Gott seine Hände euch entgegenhält.
Ihr dürft hinaus. Es wartet eine Welt."

and adults in amazement just look.
But the children come running from all directions
seeking refuge with him as their home,
and they listen to his words that are spreading
as white wings that are wide and warm.

"Have any of you ever thought about
how quickly you are pulled ashore
with every day and night that comes
through a thousand gates and doors?
The hinges are still smooth
and every gate is easily shut;
I can still help and come along,
but already your path is cut.
You reach for life, and that I am not;
you are drawn to the night, but I am the light;
you hope for joy, but I am dearth;
you long for good luck—but I am the court."
From afar the adults listened. But he turned quiet.
"You don't have to push me away," he sighed,
"when together we are taking new steps.
While you may be too young to take me along,
you can still turn around and look back,
perhaps to a modest flower garden,
perhaps to a caring mother's smile
so mild, perhaps to a longing:
For I am childhood and I am every remembering.
Give me your hand, grant me a glance in passing
while you are setting out toward life,
from which the new and never employed
God extends his hands to you.
Now a world awaits. You are free to go."

Sie horchten hastig seinem Verheißen,
ihre Wangen waren so warm:
"Werden wir an den Türen reißen?!"
ruft ein wilder Kleiner im Schwarm.
Und da bettelt er bang: "Du, führe
schnell uns weiter durch Wasser und Wald,
und die große, die letzte Türe
kommst sie dann bald?"

So an dem Glück, das der Meister verkündet,
haben sich hell seine Augen entzündet,
und er blüht in der Sonne auf.
Aber da hebt sich aus horchendem Hauf
einsam ein Kleiner, ihm weht das verworrne
welkende Haar um die Stirne gebläht
wie die zerrissene Zier überm Zorne
eines Helmes weht.
Seine Stimme flattert und fleht:
"Du!" er klammert um seine Knie
bange die armen hungernden Hände—
"Solche Worte vom ewigen Ende
sagtest du nie!
Wenn die anderen undankbaren
weiter wollen zu jagenden Jahren—
ich bin anders, anders wie sie!"
Und er umklammert im Krampfe die Knie.—

Und die Lippen des Lichten erbeben,
und er neigt sich dem Weinenden leise:
"Giebt die Mutter dir Spiel und Speise?"
Da schluchzt ihm der Knab in den Schooß:
"Zum Spielen bin ich zu groß."
"Bringt sie dir morgens ins Stübchen
deine Brühe warm?"

They hastily listened to this,
with their cheeks aglow:
"Will we be pulling hard at the doors?!"
a wild one cried from the crowd.
And then he begs: "Go ahead and lead
quickly through water and woods;
and are we there at the final door
anytime soon?"

At the news the master had told
the eyes of the boy rejoice,
his face alights in the sun.
But from the crowd of small listeners
a lonely boy gets up,
with wispy hair, tangled and blown,
like the trim that is torn
of a helmet of war,
and his voice with trembling implores:
"You!" he is clasping the master's knee
with poor and hungry hands—
"You never said anything at all
about life in eternity!
When the others ungratefully strive
after ever more promising years—
I am different, so different from them!"
And he clasps and grasps at his knee.

And the lips of the clear one tremble
and he bends to the crying lad:
"Does your mother feed you and play?"
But the boy weeps in his lap:
"For playing I am too big."
"In the morning, does she not make
a breakfast for you in the room?"

Da bebt das bangende Bübchen:
"Bin zum Essen zu arm."
"Küßt sie dir nie die Wange
mit ihrer Liebe rot?"
Da gesteht er: "Lange, lange
ist mir die Mutter tot." . . .
Und die Lippen des Lichten erbeben
wie Blätter im herbstlichen Hain:
"Oh dann warst du schon draußen im Leben,
und wir können beisammen sein."

Auferweckung des Lazarus

Also, das tat not für den und den,
weil sie Zeichen brauchten, welche schrieen.
Doch er träumte, Marthen und Marieen
müßte es genügen, einzusehn, daß er könne.
Aber keiner glaubte, alle sprachen: Herr, was kommst du nun?

The boy is trembling even more:
"For eating I am too poor."
"Does she not kiss your cheek
with lips of her love that are red?"
He confesses: "For a long, long time
the mother has been dead."
And the lips of the clear one tremble
like leaves in the autumn sun:
"Then you've been already out there in life,
and we walk together as one."

Inspired by and adapted from the painting "Let the Children Come unto Me" by Fritz von Uhde. In the essay "Uhdes Christus," Rilke identified the true, living, and "eternal" Christ as the one reflected in the eyes of children as a figure of love, mercy, and refuge. In this Christ, Uhde had given them "a father without the worries, the aging process, the anger a father has, in short, a fulfillment for the deepest and most secret longings of these little awaking souls" Uhde's later paintings of Jesus, however, lacked this spontaneity and were patterned after convention and intent to please both public and benefactor, which made clear "the lie and dishonesty" of their Christ. The occasion for this criticism is when in the summer of 1897 Uhde makes significant changes on the last in a series of Christ paintings, "Christ's Ascension," to meet the stipulations of the buyer, the Pinakothek of Munich, and to effect the painting's inclusion in the royal paintings collection. Munich, summer 1897

The Raising of Lazarus
(Poems 1906-1926)

For some it was the only way they could believe,
they needed these blaring signs.
But he had hoped that for Marthas and Marys
knowing that he could, did suffice.
Instead they said: Why are you late, Lord?

Und da ging er hin, das Unerlaubte
an der ruhigen Natur zu tun.
Zürnender. Die Augen fast geschlossen,
fragte er sie nach dem Grab. Er litt.
Ihnen schien es, seine Tränen flossen,
und sie drängten voller Neugier mit.
Noch im Gehen wars ihm ungeheuer,
ein entsetzlich spielender Versuch,
aber plötzlich brach ein hohes Feuer
in ihm aus, ein solcher Widerspruch
gegen all ihre Unterschiede,
ihr Gestorben—, ihr Lebendigsein,
daß er Feindschaft war in jedem Gliede,
als er heiser angab: Hebt den Stein!
Eine Stimme rief, daß er schon stinke,
(denn er lag den vierten Tag)—doch Er
stand gestrafft, ganz voll von jenem Winke,
welcher stieg in ihm und schwer, sehr schwer
ihm die Hand hob—(niemals hob sich eine
langsamer als diese Hand und mehr)
bis sie dastand, scheinend in der Luft;
und dort oben zog sie sich zur Kralle:
denn ihn graute jetzt, es möchten alle
Toten durch die angesaugte Gruft
wiederkommen, wo es sich herauf
raffte, larvig, aus der graden Lage—
doch dann stand nur Eines schief im Tage,
und man sah: das ungenaue, vage
Leben nahm es wieder mit in Kauf.

And so he proceeded to perform
what ran counter to nature's norm.
He was angry. With his eyes nearly shut
he inquired about the tomb. He hurt.
It appeared tears had welled up,
and inquiringly they followed along.
Even while en route he was daunted
by this terrible mocking experiment;
a sudden flame flared up in him,
which was stark opposition and dislike
of all their distinctions:
of being dead, of being alive,
and every limb in him was torn
when calling hoarsely: Move the stone!
A voice mentioned the body's stench
(since this was Day Four).
But he stood steeled, of a resolve that grew
and gravely and at great pains
made him lift his hand—
(never before was a hand so slow)
and then stopped in midair;
and up there the hand had become claw:
now he worried that all the dead,
sucked up thus, might be coming back,
reemerging larva-like from their beds—
but only one stood crooked in the day;
this life, so imprecise and vague,
let him have another stay.

John 11:1-44; the icon depicting the Raising of Lazarus is a popular one in Eastern churches. Ronda, January 1913

Der Ölbaum-Garten

Er ging hinauf unter dem grauen Laub
ganz grau und aufgelöst im Ölgelände
und legte seine Stirne voller Staub
tief in das Staubigsein der heißen Hände.

Nach allem dies. Und dieses war der Schluß.
Jetzt soll ich gehen, während ich erblinde,
und warum willst Du, daß ich sagen muß
Du seist, wenn ich Dich selber nicht mehr finde.

Ich finde Dich nicht mehr. Nicht in mir, nein.
Nicht in den andern. Nicht in diesem Stein.
Ich finde Dich nicht mehr. Ich bin allein.

Ich bin allein mit aller Menschen Gram,
den ich durch Dich zu lindern unternahm,
der Du nicht bist. O namenlose Scham. . .

Später erzählte man: Ein Engel kam—.

Warum ein Engel? Ach es kam die Nacht
und blätterte gleichgültig in den Bäumen.
Die Jünger rührten sich in ihren Träumen.
Warum ein Engel? Ach es kam die Nacht.

Die Nacht, die kam, war keine ungemeine;
so gehen hunderte vorbei.
Da schlafen Hunde und da liegen Steine.
Ach eine traurige, ach irgendeine,
die wartet, bis es wieder Morgen sei.

Mount of Olives
(New Poems, 1907)

He climbed the hill amidst the silvery leaves
so grey and grave in olive fields
and placed his forehead streaked with dust
into his sweaty palms.

So this is it. And this then was the end.
Now I am asked to leave, so blind,
and why would you desire me to say
you are, when you it is I cannot find?

I no longer find you. Within me, you are not.
Not in others. Not in this rock.
I no longer find you. I am alone.

I am alone amidst the world's pain,
which with your help I sought to abate,
you who are not, without name.

Later they said: an angel came—:

Why an angel? No, the night arrived
and ran haphazardly through the trees.
The disciples moved about in their dreams.
Why an angel? It was the night.

The night that came was nothing much;
of such a one there were a hundred before,
where the dogs sleep and the rocks rest.
It was a sad one, though just any one
that awaited the dawn.

Denn Engel kommen nicht zu solchen Betern,
und Nächte werden nicht um solche groß.
Die sich Verlierenden läßt alles los,
und sie sind preisgegeben von den Vätern
und ausgeschlossen aus der Mütter Schooß.

Das Abendmahl

Sie sind versammelt, staunende Verstörte,
um ihn, der wie ein Weiser sich beschließt
und der sich fortnimmt denen er gehörte
und der an ihnen fremd vorüberfließt.
Die alte Einsamkeit kommt über ihn,
die ihn erzog zu seinem tiefen Handeln;
nun wird er wieder durch den Ölwald wandeln,
und die ihn lieben werden vor ihm fliehn.

Er hat sie zu dem letzten Tisch entboten
und (wie ein Schuß die Vögel aus den Schoten
scheucht) scheucht er ihre Hände aus den Broten
mit seinem Wort: sie fliegen zu ihm her;
sie flattern bange durch die Tafelrunde
und suchen einen Ausgang. Aber er
ist überall wie eine Dämmerstunde.

Angels don't come to praying ones like these
and their nights don't turn out to be famous and great.
Those who lose themselves are completely alone,
are abandoned by their fathers
and locked out of their mothers' womb.

*Of the Synoptic Gospels only Luke 22:39-46 mentions an angel
ministering to Jesus, Matthew 26:36-46 and Mark 14:32-42 do not.
Possibly inspired by El Greco's "Christ at the Mount of Olives."
Paris, May-June 1906.*

Last Supper
(The Book of Images, 1902/06)

They are gathered, amazed and confused,
around him, who is closed up like a sage
withholding what once belonged to them
and strangely absent and grave.
This ancient loneliness comes over him,
which had been feeding his every act;
again he is walking through the field of olives,
from where those who loved him fled.

He called them to the final meal
and (like a shot rousing birds from shrubs)
he sweeps their hands from loaf and crust
with words: they fly to him;
they flutter round the meal
and seek a door. But he
is everywhere like dusk.

*Luke 22:14-16; inspired by Leonardo da Vinci's famous fresco,
which Rilke saw in the original a year after writing the poem in the
summer of 1904. The agitation of the disciples and their moving
hands expressed in the fresco is reiterated in the poem. Paris, June
1903.*

Kreuzigung

Längst geübt, zum kahlen Galgenplatze
irgend ein Gesindel zu gedrängen,
ließen sich die schweren Knechte hängen,
dann und wann nur eine große Fratze

kehrend nach den abgetanen Drein.
Aber oben war das schlechte Henkern
rasch abgetan; und nach dem Fertigsein
ließen sich die freien Männer schlenkern.

Bis der eine (fleckig wie ein Selcher)
sagte: Hauptmann, dieser hat geschrien.
Und der Hauptmann sah vom Pferde: Welcher?
und es war ihm selber, er hätte ihn

den Elia rufen hören. Alle
waren zuzuschauen voller Lust,
und sie hielten, daß er nicht verfalle,
gierig ihm die ganze Essiggalle
an sein schwindendes Gehust.

Denn sie hofften noch ein ganzes Spiel
und vielleicht den kommenden Elia.
Aber hinten ferne schrie Maria,
und er selber brüllte und verfiel.

Crucifixion
(Of the New Poems' Other Part, 1908)

Well versed in the art of shoving
the hoodlums to the gallows' site,
the sturdy hangmen were letting it all hang out
by cutting an ugly face at them,

at the threesome they had hung.
Since above their heads this shoddy hanging
was a deal now done;
the free men below carried on.

Until one (with blotches like smoked meat)
said: O Captain, this one screamed.
And the captain on the horse asked, Which?
though he thought he figured which

had screamed "Elijah" then. For all
had watched with great delight, when one
held up the bitter wine to keep
from dying—him who greedily
sucked up the sour sap.

For they had hoped to keep him alive
for another round of gambling, or Elijah perhaps.
But from a distance, in back, Mary cried,
and he issued a loud scream and died.

*Matthew 27:33-56; in 1893 in Prague the eighteen-year-old Rilke
had composed a poem titled "Christ at the Cross," which was found
after his death. In it Rilke suggests that Jesus was killed because of
his precipitous claim to be more than a human being. Paris, summer
1908*

Christi Höllenfahrt

Endlich verlitten, entging sein Wesen dem schrecklichen
Leibe der Leiden. Oben. Ließ ihn.
Und die Finsternis fürchtete sich allein
und warf an das Bleiche
Fledermäuse heran,—immer noch schwankt abends
in ihrem Flattern die Angst vor dem Aufprall
an die erkaltete Qual. Dunkle ruhlose Luft
entmutigte sich an dem Leichnam; und in den starken
wachsamen Tieren der Nacht war Dumpfheit und Unlust.
Sein entlassener Geist gedachte vielleicht in der Landschaft
anzustehen, unhandelnd. Denn seiner Leidung Ereignis
war noch genug. Maßvoll
schien ihm der Dinge nächtliches Dastehn,
und wie ein trauriger Raum griff er darüber um sich.
Aber die Erde, vertrocknet im Durst seiner Wunden,
aber die Erde riß auf, und es rufte im Abgrund.
Er, Kenner der Martern, hörte die Hölle
herheulend, begehrend Bewußtsein
seiner vollendeten Not: daß über dem Ende der seinen
(unendlichen) ihre, während Pein erschrecke, ahne.
Und er stürzte, der Geist, mit der völligen Schwere
seiner Erschöpfung herein: schritt als ein Eilender
durch das befremdete Nachschaun weidender Schatten,
hob zu Adam den Aufblick, eilig,
eilte hinab, schwand, schien und verging in dem Stürzen
wilderer Tiefen. Plötzlich (höher höher) über der Mitte
aufschäumender Schreie, auf dem langen
Turm seines Duldens trat er hervor: ohne Atem,
stand, ohne Geländer, Eigentümer der Schmerzen. Schwieg.

Christ's Descent into Hell
(Poems 1906-1926)

At last dead, his entire being did escape the horrid
body of his suffering. Above. Was released.
And the night was afraid of itself
and hurled at the pale corpse its bats,—
there still is in their wings' fluttering at night
the fear to collide
with this cold body. Dark and agitated air
wore itself out on it; and the animals of the night,
so strong and alert, grow dull and inert.
Perhaps his released spirit thought of lingering about,
passive. For it still was too torn by the pain.
There was plenty to digest in the dark,
and his soul groped about above.
But the earth, so drained and parched by the wounds,
this earth tore apart, and voices came up.
He, who knew all the martyrs, could hear the sounds of hell,
howling, wanting to be seen for its perfected despair:
also, to frighten and to indicate the everlasting pain of theirs.
And so, this spirit of his
plunged with all the weight of its exhaustion into the abyss:
strode quickly past the curious glances of the shadows there,
glanced at Adam, with haste, and proceeded
hurriedly downward, emerged and disappeared in the floods
of even deeper depths. But suddenly (higher, much higher up),
above the tossing and rising of screams,
he resurfaced as if by his suffering buoyed:
he stood, breathless, unpropped, owner of every pain,
and was quiet.

*According to the Apostles' Creed, Christ descended into the outermost
fringes of hell between his death and resurrection. The doctrine, also called
Christ's Harrowing of Hell, was formulated after the fourth century and is*

Der Auferstandene

Er vermochte niemals bis zuletzt
ihr zu weigern oder abzuneinen,
daß sie ihrer Liebe sich berühme;
und sie sank ans Kreuz in dem Kostüme
eines Schmerzes, welches ganz besetzt
war mit ihrer Liebe größten Steinen.

Aber da sie dann, um ihn zu salben,
an das Grab kam, Tränen im Gesicht,
war er auferstanden ihrethalben,
daß er seliger ihr sage: Nicht—

Sie begriff es erst in ihrer Höhle,
wie er ihr, gestärkt durch seinen Tod,
endlich das Erleichternde der Öle
und des Rührens Vorgefühl verbot,

derived from such scripture passages as Matthew 27:52f; Rom. 10:6-8; Eph. 4:8-10; I Peter 3:18-20. Various reasons have been given for Christ's descent: Christ went to hell to bring back the souls of the just who had died before his coming; Christ preached to the departed and brought back those who responded; and Christ conquered the citadel of Satan and set its captives free (Luther). Calvin held that the phrase was to be understood in a spiritual sense, namely that Christ "suffered in his soul the dreadful torments of a person condemned and irretrievably lost." Rilke touches upon Calvin's view. The icon of Christ's descent into hell and his resurrection, called anastasis, is a staple in Byzantine art and in the Eastern church; it constitutes the church's Easter image, showing Christ breaking down the gates of hell and releasing Old Testament figures. Written in Paris, April 1913.

The Risen One
(Of the New Poems' Other Part, 1908)

Even at the end he could never bring himself
to refuse or deny her the privilege
of demonstrating her love for him;
and so, at the cross, he allowed her to cling
and to wear the robe of her suffering,
studded with the stones of her love.

But when she arrived at the grave
so as to embalm him, with tears on her face,
he had risen for her sake
and could tell her at last to stop:

She only understood when alone
that his death had steeled her and forbade
the sentimental urge to sob and cling,
as this most soothing balm of old.

um aus ihr die Liebende zu formen
die sich nicht mehr zum Geliebten neigt,
weil sie, hingerissen von enormen
Stürmen, seine Stimme übersteigt.

Emmaus

Noch nicht im Gehn; obwohl er seltsam sicher
zu ihnen trat, für ihren Gang bereit;
und ob er gleich die Schwelle feierlicher
hinüberschritt als sie die Männlichkeit;
noch nicht, da man sich um den Tisch verteilte,
beschämlich niederstellend das und dies,
und er, wie duldend, seine unbeeilte
Zuschauerschaft auf ihnen ruhen ließ;
selbst nicht, da man sich setzte, willens nun,
sich gastlich an einander zu gewöhnen,
und er das Brot ergriff, mit seinen schönen
zögernden Händen, um jetzt das zu tun,
was jene, wie den Schrecken einer Menge,
durchstürzte mit unendlichem Bezug—
da endlich, sehender, wie er die Enge
der Mahlzeit gebend auseinanderschlug:
erkannten sie. Und, zitternd hochgerissen,
standen sie krumm und hatten bange lieb.
Dann, als sie sahen, wie er gebend blieb,
langten sie bebend nach den beiden Bissen.

Now he had made her one who was loving,
not just to the lover pulled and drawn;
and having been shaken by vicious storms
she had come into her own.

John 20:11-17; Mary Magdalene, who had come to embalm Jesus'
body, encounters the risen Christ and is told by him to stop clinging.
As visual model, Rilke had used Rodin's Pietá of Jesus and Mary
Magdalene, on which is based the 1906 poem Pieta included in New
Poems; here, however, Mary's pain leads to self-transcendence and an
autonomy of authentic living expressed in an ethics of love. Paris, fall
1907 or Capri, spring 1908

Emmaeus
(Poems 1906-1926)

Not while walking, even though he stepped
so strangely resolute up to them, ready for the walk;
and even though he had stepped up with greater dignity
than they had stepped up to their virility;
not while gathering around the table
and placing on it with embarrassment this and that,
while he, so willingly, remained a spectator
calmly resting his eyes on them;
not even when sitting down, and finally ready
to get acquainted through this act of hospitality,
where he took the bread into his hands
with care and with hesitation so as to do
that which burst upon them, like terror upon a crowd,
and was of utmost significance—
only when they saw how he broke open
the constraints of the bread he gave:
that they recognized him. And, pulled to their feet,
they swerved awkwardly into a fearful embrace.
And when they saw that while giving he stayed,
they shakily reached for both halves.

Luke 24:28-32; Paris, April 1913

IV. Von der Pilgerschaft

Der Schutzengel

Du bist der Vogel, dessen Flügel kamen,
wenn ich erwachte in der Nacht und rief.
Nur mit den Armen rief ich, denn dein Namen
ist wie ein Abgrund, tausend Nächte tief.
Du bist der Schatten, drin ich still entschlief,
und jeden Traum ersinnt in mir dein Samen,—
du bist das Bild, ich aber bin der Rahmen,
der dich ergänzt in glänzendem Relief.

Wie nenn ich dich? Sieh, meine Lippen lahmen.
Du bist der Anfang, der sich groß ergießt,
ich bin das langsame und bange Amen,
das deine Schönheit scheu beschließt.

Du hast mich oft aus dunklem Ruhn gerissen,
wenn mir das Schlafen wie ein Grab erschien
und wie Verlorengehen und Entfliehn,—
da hobst du mich aus Herzensfinsternissen
und wolltest mich auf allen Türmen hissen
wie Scharlachfahnen und wie Draperien.

Du: der von Wundern redet wie vom Wissen
und von den Menschen wie von Melodien
und von den Rosen: von Ereignissen,
die flammend sich in deinem Blick vollziehn,—
du Seliger, wann nennst du einmal Ihn,
aus dessen siebentem und letztem Tage
noch immer Glanz auf deinem Flügelschlage
verloren liegt. . .
Befiehlst du, daß ich frage?

IV. The Pilgrimage

The Guardian Angel
(The Book of Images, 1902/06– "The First Book's First Part")

You are the bird whose wings appeared
when I awoke at night and called.
I used my arms to call you, since
your name lies far and deep.
You are the shade that made me sleep,
and every dream is due to you—
you are the image, I the frame
that makes you look complete.

What do I call you? See, my lips debate.
You are the beginning that spills over all,
I am the hesitant, timid closing,
the "amen" of your beautiful state.

You often tore me out of darkest nights,
when sleep appeared like lying in a grave
and being lost and running from it all—
that's when you lifted me from my despair
and had me hoisted high on wall and pole
like bunting or like scarlet flags.

You who talk about miracles as if they were facts
and of people as if melodies
and of roses as if of occurrences
that flare up whenever you look—:
when will you name Him whose glorious rays
issued from the seventh and ultimate day
and still dimly shimmer upon your wing
and nearly have gone . . .
Are these, my questions or your command?

Berlin-Schmargendorf, July 1899

Engellieder

Ich ließ meinen Engel lange nicht los,
und er verarmte mir in den Armen
und wurde klein, und ich wurde groß:
und auf einmal war ich das Erbarmen,
und er eine zitternde Bitte bloß.

Da hab ich ihm seine Himmel gegeben,—
und er ließ mir das Nahe, daraus er entschwand;
er lernte das Schweben, ich lernte das Leben,
und wir haben langsam einander erkannt. . .

Seit mich mein Engel nicht mehr bewacht,
kann er frei seine Flügel entfalten
und die Stille der Sterne durchspalten,—
denn er muß meiner einsamen Nacht
nicht mehr die ängstlichen Hände halten—
seit mich mein Engel nicht mehr bewacht.

Hat auch mein Engel keine Pflicht mehr,
seit ihn mein strenger Tag vertrieb,
oft senkt er sehnend sein Gesicht her
und hat die Himmel nicht mehr lieb.

Er möchte wieder aus armen Tagen
über der Wälder rauschendem Ragen
meine blassen Gebete tragen
in die Heimat der Cherubim.

Dorthin trug er mein frühes Weinen
und Bedanken, und meine kleinen

Angel Songs
(In Celebration of Me, 1909)

For a long time I clung to my guardian angel,
and he grew tired in my arms and lame
and became so small, while I grew big;
suddenly I was the one granting mercy,
and he the one seeking it.

So I gave him back his heavens—
and he let me have everything nearby;
he learned to soar and I learned to live
and we honored the other's ways.

Since my angel need no longer stand guard
he can freely spread his wings
and cut through the milky ways of the stars—
and need not hold the trembling hands
of my lonely nights,
since my angel need no longer stand guard.

Even though my angel no longer has duties
since my life has shooed him away,
he often looks over to me with longing
and at the heavens he looks with disdain.

He would like to carry from days of gloom
my prayers that were so dim
across the forests of rustling leaves
to the dwelling of cherubim.

There he took my former thanks and pleas,
and all my little sorrows grew

Leiden wuchsen dorten zu Hainen,
welche flüstern über ihm. . .

Wenn ich einmal im Lebensland,
im Gelärme von Markt und Messe—
meiner Kindheit erblühte Blässe:
meinen ernsten Engel vergesse—
seine Güte und sein Gewand,
die betenden Hände, die segnende Hand,—
in meinen heimlichsten Träumen behalten
werde ich immer das Flügelfalten,
das wie eine weiße Zypresse
hinter ihm stand. . .

Seine Hände blieben wie blinde
Vögel, die, um die Sonne betrogen,
wenn die andern über die Wogen
zu den währenden Lenzen zogen,
in der leeren, entlaubten Linde
wehren müssen dem Winterwinde.

Auf seinen Wangen war die Scham
der Bräute, die über der Seele Schrecken
dunkle Purpurdecken
breiten dem Bräutigam.

Und in den Augen lag
Glanz von dem ersten Tag,—
aber weit über allem war
ragend das tragende Flügelpaar. . .

like groves so vast
and they whispered to him . . . .

Even if at times in this course of life,
the din of fairs and the market place—
I forget my devout angel
of a childhood now passed—
his mercy, his garb,
my folded hands, his benediction—
I will always, in my innermost being, recall
the folding of his wings,
so white, which like a cypress tree
loomed tall . . . .

His hands are like birds that cannot see
and have been deprived of the sun,
and while others continue to migrate
to regions that prolong the spring,
his hands have to fend off the winter's cold
amidst barren and leafless trees.

Upon his cheeks was written the shame
of brides afraid in their room
spreading dark purple covers
for the arrival of the groom.

And in the eyes was reflected
the gleam of the very first day—
but above everything loomed
the wings that could bear one away . . . .

Um die vielen Madonnen sind
viele ewige Engelknaben,
die Verheißung und Heimat haben
in dem Garten, wo Gott beginnt.
Und sie ragen alle nach Rang,
und sie tragen die goldenen Geigen,
und die Schönsten dürfen nie schweigen:
ihre Seelen sind aus Gesang.
Immer wieder müssen sie
klingen alle die dunkeln Chorale,
die sie klangen vieltausend Male:
Gott stieg nieder aus seinem Strahle
und du warst die schönste Schale
Seiner Sehnsucht, Madonna Marie.

Aber oft in der Dämmerung
wird die Mutter müder und müder,—
und dann flüstern die Engelbrüder,
und sie jubeln sie wieder jung.
Und sie winken mit den weißen
Flügeln festlich im Hallenhofe,
und sie heben aus den heißen
Herzen höher die eine Strophe:
Alle, die in Schönheit gehn,
werden in Schönheit auferstehn.

≈

Around the many madonnas
hover everlasting angelic beings,
which have their home and calling
in the garden where God begins.
And they all scramble for status,
and they carry their violins of gold,
and the prettiest may never be silent
for their souls carry praise songs of old.
Forever they have to be resounding
the mysterious choral pieces and chants
they have been performing for millennia: And
as a result, God descends from above
with you, Holy Virgin, becoming the receiving
vessel of his longing and love.

But at times, when the sun has gone down,
the Virgin is so tired and worn—
and then the angels conspire
to cheer her up and revive her.
And from the courtyard they raise
festively their wings in praise,
and they gather up in one accord
these heartfelt words:
All who walk in beauty here,
in beauty they will reappear.

*The Angel Songs were written in February 1898 in Berlin, except for
the last two stanzas, composed in April 1898 in Florence; these last
stanzas were inspired by early Renaissance paintings of madonnas
seen in Florence of which Rilke makes mention in his Florentine
Diary.*

Strophen

Ist einer, der nimmt alle in die Hand,
daß sie wie Sand durch seine Finger rinnen.
Er wählt die schönsten aus den Königinnen
und läßt sie sich in weißen Marmor hauen,
still liegend in des Mantels Melodie;
und legt die Könige zu ihren Frauen,
gebildet aus dem gleichen Stein wie sie.

Ist einer, der nimmt alle in die Hand,
daß sie wie schlechte Klingen sind und brechen.
Er ist kein Fremder, denn er wohnt im Blut,
das unser Leben ist und rauscht und ruht.
Ich kann nicht glauben, daß er Unrecht tut;
doch hör ich viele Böses von ihm sprechen.

Der Reliquienschrein

Draussen wartete auf alle Ringe
und auf jedes Kettenglied
Schicksal, das nicht ohne sie geschieht.
Drinnen waren sie nur Dinge, Dinge
die er schmiedete; denn vor dem Schmied
war sogar die Krone, die er bog,
nur ein Ding, ein zitterndes und eines
das er finster wie im Zorn erzog
zu dem Tragen eines reinen Steines.

Stanzas

(The Book of Images, 1902/06—"The First Book's Second Part")

There is one in charge of them all,
so they sift through his fingers like sand.
He chooses for queens the prettiest ones
and has them in whitest marble carved,
enveloping them in melodies' tunes:
and placing the kings right next to them
hewn from the same marble stone.

There is one in charge of them all,
so they make for dull blades and break.
But he is no stranger to us for he lives
in this our life that flows and ebbs.
I can't believe him unjust, although
many regard him as that.

Between 1900 and 1902; originally called "Der Kahn" ("The Boat"
[1900]) and based on Heinrich Vogeler's painting "Juni-Nacht"
("June Night").

The Reliquary
(Of the New Poems' Other Part, 1908)

Outside was waiting for all the rings
and every chain link providence,
which cannot approach without their aid.
But inside they only were things, the things
he molded and made; the goldsmith saw
the crown—even that, he sought to bend
as merely a trembling thing he wrought
and trained with gruff and angry force
to hold a radiant gem.

Seine Augen wurden immer kälter
von dem kalten täglichen Getränk;
aber als der herrliche Behälter
(goldgetrieben, köstlich, vielkarätig)
fertig vor ihm stand, das Weihgeschenk,
daß darin ein kleines Handgelenk
fürder wohne, weiß und wundertätig:

blieb er ohne Ende auf den Knien,
hingeworfen, weinend, nichtmehr wagend,
seine Seele niederschlagend
vor dem ruhigen Rubin,
der ihn zu gewahren schien
und ihn, plötzlich um sein Dasein fragend,
ansah wie aus Dynastien.

Béguinage
Béguinage Sainte-Elisabeth, Brügge

I.

Das hohe Tor scheint keine einzuhalten,
die Brücke geht gleich gerne hin und her,
und doch sind sicher alle in dem alten
offenen Ulmenhof und gehn nicht mehr
aus ihren Häusern, als auf jenem Streifen
zur Kirche hin, um besser zu begreifen
warum in ihnen so viel Liebe war.

Dort knieen sie, verdeckt mit reinem Leinen,

His eyes grew ever colder from use
in the daily dross of applying his skill;
but when the container, so beautiful
(resplendent and rich and of solid gold)
was formed and stood, as sacred gift,
before him to store the little wrist,
the white and wondrous relic of old:

he fell to his knees and remained for long
prostrate, in tears, no longer resisting,
and all of his being surrendering
before this ruby, so quiet and calm,
which had appeared to take note of him
and asked him about the life he lived
with eyes as from dynasties.

*Reliquaries, displayed for veneration in Roman Catholic and Eastern
churches, were containers of precious metal or sculpted wood containing remains of saints or sacred objects. Drafts and provisional version
Paris, August 5, 1907; final version probably August 1908, Paris.*

The Beguinage
(Of the New Poems' Other Part, 1908)

I.

The high gate appears to keep none of them in;
the bridge would gladly lead back and forth,
but nonetheless they all surely are
back there in the old and wide elm yard,
and don't leave their houses but for a walk
on that path to church as to comprehend
why so much love is in them.

Inside they kneel in pure linen concealed,

so gleich, als wäre nur das Bild der einen
tausendmal im Choral, der tief und klar
zu Spiegeln wird an den verteilten Pfeilern;
und ihre Stimmen gehn den immer steilern
Gesang hinan und werfen sich von dort,
wo es nicht weitergeht, vom letzten Wort,
den Engeln zu, die sie nicht wiedergeben.

Drum sind die unten, wenn sie sich erheben
und wenden, still. Drum reichen sie sich schweigend
mit einem Neigen, Zeigende zu zeigend
Empfangenden, geweihtes Wasser, das
die Stirnen kühl macht und die Munde blaß.

Und gehen dann, verhangen und verhalten,
auf jenem Streifen wieder überquer—
die Jungen ruhig, ungewiß die Alten
und eine Greisin, weilend, hinterher—
zu ihren Häusern, die sie schnell verschweigen
und die sich durch die Ulmen hin von Zeit
zu Zeit ein wenig reine Einsamkeit,
 in einer kleine Scheibe schimmernd, zeigen.

II.

Was aber spiegelt mit den tausend Scheiben
das Kirchenfenster in den Hof hinein,
darin sich Schweigen, Schein und Widerschein
vermischen, trinken, trüben, übertreiben,
phantastisch alternd wie ein alter Wein.

Dort legt sich, keiner weiß von welcher Seite,
Außen auf Inneres und Ewigkeit
auf Immer-Hingehn, Weite über Weite,
erblindend, finster, unbenutzt, verbleit.

identical all, as if one was mirrored
a thousandfold in the high choir loft and
again below amidst spaced-out pillars;
and their voices ascend ever steeper scales
and once at the top with nowhere to go
they hurl themselves into the angels' lap
with the angels not giving them back.

It is the reason the women below,
when rising and turning, are very still;
and silently they dispense with a bow,
at once those who give and those who receive,
the holy water on foreheads and lips.

And then they walk calmly and with restraint
on the very path that cuts across—
the young ones straight, the old ones not,
with an older woman that has fallen behind—
back to their houses that quickly conceal
and only reveal from between the trees
a fleeting piece of pure solitude
that shines through a small window frame.

II.

But with a thousand panels of glass
the church window mirrors into the yard
the silence, radiance, reflection,
which it mixes, absorbs, makes dim, enlarges,
and magically ages like wine.

Then there arrives, no one knows from where,
the external and settles on what lives within;
eternity settles upon a routine
that's blinding, leaded, unwieldy, and dark.

Dort bleibt, unter dem schwankenden Dekor
des Sommertags, das Graue alter Winter:
als stünde regungslos ein sanftgesinnter
langmütig lange Wartender dahinter
und eine weinend Wartende davor.

Der Schauende

Ich sehe den Bäumen die Stürme an,
die aus laugewordenen Tagen
an meine ängstlichen Fenster schlagen,
und höre die Fernen Dinge sagen,
die ich nicht ohne Freund ertragen,
nicht ohne Schwester lieben kann.

Da geht der Sturm, ein Umgestalter,
geht durch den Wald und durch die Zeit,
und alles ist wie ohne Alter:
die Landschaft, wie ein Vers im Psalter,
ist Ernst und Wucht und Ewigkeit.

Wie ist das klein, womit wir ringen,
was mit uns ringt, wie ist es groß;

There lingers, beneath the trembling decor
of a summer's day, the old winter's grey:
as if there stood calmly a gently disposed
patiently waiting groom in back,
while up front one waited and wept.

The Beguines (women) and Beghards (men) were a semimonastic
movement of the church begun in the 12th and 13th centuries in
Belgium, the Netherlands, and Germany. It involved mostly women
who, without taking solemn vows and becoming nuns, lived in commu-
nity housing and practiced celibacy, were devoted to a life of poverty,
and engaged in regular liturgical prayer, sacramental practice, and
works of mercy. Rilke wrote the poem in Paris, July 19-20, 1907,
having visited the beguinage of Sainte-Elisabeth, at Brügge or Bruge,
in Belgium.

The Observer
(The Book of Images, 1902/1906– "The Second Book's
Second Part")

I can tell a storm by the way the trees
are whipping, compared to when quiet,
against my trembling windows, and
I hear from afar things whispering
I couldn't bear hearing without a friend
or love without a sister close by.

There moves the storm, the transforming one,
and runs through the woods and through the age,
changing it all to look ageless and young:
the landscape appears like the verse of a psalm,
so earnest, eternal, and strong.

How small is what we contend with and fight;
how great what contends with us;

ließen wir, ähnlicher den Dingen,
uns so vom großen Sturm bezwingen,—
wir würden weit und namenlos.

Was wir besiegen, ist das Kleine,
und der Erfolg selbst macht uns klein.
Das Ewige und Ungemeine
will nicht von uns gebogen sein.
Das ist der Engel, der den Ringern
des Alten Testaments erschien:
wenn seiner Widersacher Sehnen
im Kampfe sich metallen dehnen,
fühlt er sie unter seinen Fingern
wie Saiten tiefer Melodien.

Wen dieser Engel überwand,
welcher so oft auf Kampf verzichtet,
der geht gerecht und aufgerichtet
und groß aus jener harten Hand,
die sich, wie formend, an ihn schmiegte.
Die Siege laden ihn nicht ein.
Sein Wachstum ist: der Tiefbesiegte
von immer Größerem zu sein.

if only we mirrored the moves of the things
and acquiesced to the force of the storm,
we, too, could be ageless and strong.

For what we can conquer is only the small,
and winning itself turns us into dwarfs;
but the everlasting and truly important
will never be conquered by us.
It is the angel who made himself known
to the wrestlers of the Old Testament:
for whenever he saw his opponents propose
to test their iron-clad muscle strength,
he touched them like strings of an instrument
and played their low-sounding chords.

Whoever submits to this angel,
whoever refuses to fight the fight,
comes out walking straight and great and upright,
and the hand once rigid and hard
shapes around as a gently curved guard.
No longer is winning a tempting bait.
One's progress is to be conquered, instead,
by the ever mightier one.

Originally called "Sturm" ("Storm"); the poem makes reference to Jacob's struggle with the angel in Genesis 32:25-33; Berlin-Schmargendorf, January 1901.

Ernste Stunde

Wer jetzt weint irgendwo in der Welt,
>> ohne Grund weint in der Welt,
>> weint über mich.

Wer jetzt lacht irgendwo in der Nacht,
>> ohne Grund lacht in der Nacht,
>> lacht mich aus.

Wer jetzt geht irgendwo in der Welt,
>> ohne Grund geht in der Welt,
>> geht zu mir.

Wer jetzt stirbt irgendwo in der Welt,
>> ohne Grund stirbt in der Welt:
>> sieht mich an.

Die Versuchung

Nein, es half nicht, daß er sich die scharfen
Stacheln einhieb in das geile Fleisch;
alle seine trächtigen Sinne warfen
unter kreißendem Gekreisch

Frühgeburten: schiefe, hingeschielte
kriechende und fliegende Gesichte,
Nichte, deren nur auf ihn erpichte
Bosheit sich verband und mit ihm spielte.

Serious Hour
(The Book of Images, 1902/06– "The First Book's
Second Part")

Someone crying now somewhere in the world,
    without any reason or rhyme,
    cries now for me.

Someone smiling now somewhere in the night,
    without any reason or rhyme,
    laughs now at me.

Someone walking now somewhere in the world,
    without any reason or rhyme,
    walks toward me.

Someone dying now somewhere in the world,
    without any reason or rhyme,
    looks at me now.

*Due to a torn-out page in the notebooks, the first two stanzas preced-
ing the poem are missing; however, they are preceded by a longer reflection on God, which suggests that the speaker of "Serious Hour" is
God. Berlin-Schmargendorf, October 1900.*

Temptation
(Of the New Poems' Other Part, 1908)

It was useless driving sharp pricks
into the raging flesh;
all his pregnant desires were
premature births

amidst the screeching screams
of crooked and cross-eyed images,
a creeping and sweeping, the evil of which
entangled and played games with him.

Und schon hatten seine Sinne Enkel;
denn das Pack war fruchtbar in der Nacht
und in immer bunterem Gesprenkel
hingehudelt und verhundertfacht.

Aus dem Ganzen ward ein Trunk gemacht:
seine Hände griffen lauter Henkel,
und der Schatten schob sich auf wie Schenkel
warm und zu Umarmungen erwacht—.

Und da schrie er nach dem Engel, schrie:
Und der Engel kam in seinem Schein
und war da: und jagte sie
wieder in den Heiligen hinein,

daß er mit Geteufel und Getier
in sich weiterringe wie seit Jahren
und sich Gott, den lange noch nicht klaren,
innen aus dem Jäsen destillier.

An den Engel

Starker, stiller, an den Rand gestellter
Leuchter: oben wird die Nacht genau.
Wir ver-geben uns in unerhellter
Zögerung an deinem Unterbau.

Unser ist: den Ausgang nicht zu wissen
aus dem drinnen irrlichen Bezirk,
du erscheinst auf unsern Hindernissen
und beglühst sie wie ein Hochgebirg.

And already his senses bore offspring;
for this trash had mated at night
and in ever more colorful dottings
had doodled and multiplied.

And out of it all did bubble a drink:
his hands only grasped for the stems,
and its shadow unfolded like thighs,
so warm and prepared to cling—

And so he cried for the angel, screamed:
and the angel came up to his side
and was right there: and chased them all
back into the saint,

so he could again wrestle with devils and beasts
as he did in the years before,
and God, who was still rather dim in him,
could distill from the raging some more.

Possibly derived from themes of paintings by Hieronymus Bosch and Pieter Brueghel; Paris, August 21, 1907.

To the Angel
(Poems 1906-1926)

Strong and calm one, lamp by the edge:
above you the night shines clear,
while we waste ourselves in unenlightened
hesitation below your knee.

It is our lot not to know the way out
from internal confusing terrain,
while you appear atop our problems
and illumine their mountainous chain.

Deine Lust ist über unserm Reiche,
und wir fassen kaum den Niederschlag;
wie die reine Nacht der Frühlingsgleiche
stehst du teilend zwischen Tag und Tag.

Wer vermöchte je dir einzuflößen
von der Mischung, die uns heimlich trübt?
Du hast Herrlichkeit von allen Größen,
und wir sind am Kleinlichsten geübt.

Wenn wir weinen, sind wir nichts als rührend,
wo wir anschaun sind wir höchstens wach;
unser Lächeln ist nicht weit verführend,
und verführt es selbst, wer geht ihm nach?

Irgendeiner. Engel, klag ich, klag ich?
Doch wie wäre denn die Klage mein?
Ach, ich schreie, mit zwei Hölzern schlag ich
und ich meine nicht, gehört zu sein.

Daß ich lärme, wird an mir nicht lauter,
wenn du mich nicht fühltest, weil ich bin.
Leuchte, leuchte! Mach mich angeschauter
bei den Sternen. Denn ich schwinde hin.

Your bliss lives far away from us;
and we barely see it drizzle down;
like the winter night and the one in spring,
you part your day from ours.

Who could ever infuse in you
the mixture that spoils our joys?
You are versed in splendors of any size,
but the smallest is reserved as ours.

When we cry, we are only mildly touching,
whenever we look we are barely aware;
even our smile is not very alluring,
and if it allures, who cares?

Someone. Angel, am I complaining?
But how could this complaint be my own?
Yes, I am crying, and two sticks I am beating,
for I perceive not to be heard at all.

And my noises leave no mark on you
unless you acknowledge that I do exist.
Shine bright, so the stars will look at me!
I have nearly dissolved into mist.

Ronda, January 14, 1913

Nonnen-Klage

I.

Herr Jesus—geh, vergleiche
dich irgend einem Mann.
Nun bist du doch der Reiche,
nun hast du Gottes weiche
Herrlichkeiten an.

Die dir erwählt gewesen,
jetzt kostest du sie aus
und kannst mit ihnen lesen
und spielen und Theresen
zeigen dein schönes Haus.

Deine Mutter ist eine Dame
im Himmel geworden, und
ihr gekrönter Name
blüht aus unserm Mund

in diesem Wintergarten,
nach dem du zuweilen siehst,
weil du dir große Arten
aus unseren Stimmen ziehst.

II.

Herr Jesus—du hast alle
Frauen, die du nur willst.
Was liegt an meinem Schalle,
ob du ihn nimmst und stillst.

Er verliert sich im Geräusche,
er zerrinnt wie nichts im Raum.

Elegy of a Nun
(Poems 1906-1926)

I.

Lord Jesus—just look and compare
yourself to any other man.
Are you not the richest,
who wears the ever so soft
glories of God?

Those chosen by you
you can now thoroughly enjoy
and with them you can play games
and read and frolic
and share your beautiful place.

And your mother was crowned
a heavenly lady,
with a name that adorns
our mouth

in this wintry garden
at which you occasionally gaze,
because you draw from our voices
heavenly praise.

II.

Lord Jesus, you could have
any woman you please.
Why bother with me when you can
take me or leave?

My song dissipates in space
and gets lost in other noise.

Was du hörst sind andre; täusche
dich nicht: ich reiche kaum

unten aus meinem Herzen
bis in mein Gesicht, das singt.
Ich würde dich gerne schmerzen,
aber mir mißlingt

der Wurf, sooft ich mein Weh
werfe nach deinem Bilde;
es fällt von nahe milde
zurück und kalt wie Schnee.

III.

Wenn ich draußen stünde,
wo ich begonnen war,
so wären die Nächte Sünde
und der Tag Gefahr.

Es hätte mich einer genommen
und wieder gelassen, und
wäre ein zweiter gekommen
und hätte meinen Mund

verbogen mit seinen Küssen,
und dem dritten hätt ich vielleicht
barfuß folgen müssen
und hätte ihn nie erreicht;

und hätte den vierten nur so
aus Müdigkeit eingelassen,
um irgendwas zu fassen,
um zu liegen irgendwo.

What you hear are just the others:
not my voice.

I barely reach from below my heart
up to my own chin.
I would gladly hand you my pain,
but cannot win.

My pitch misses
as I aim toward you;
my pain rolls back to me slowly
and cold like snow.

III.

If I were still an outsider
and far away,
the night would be sin laden
and a danger the day.

There someone would have taken me
and then departed,
and a second one with his kisses
my lips contorted,

and a third one I might have
had to follow on bare feet,
and though trying
would never have reached;

and a fourth one I might have
out of weariness let in
to have someone to lie next to
and to cling to at least some thing.

Nun da ich bei keinem schlief,
sag: hab ich nichts begangen?
Wo war ich, während wir sangen?
Wen rief ich, wenn ich dich rief?

IV.

Mein Leben ging—Herr Jesus.
Sag mir, Herr Jesus, wohin?
Hast du es kommen sehen?
Bin ich in dir drin?
Bin ich in dir, Herr Jesus?

Denk, so kann es vergehn
mit dem täglichen Schalle.
Am Ende leugnen es alle,
keiner hat es gesehn.
War es das meine, Herr Jesus?

War es wirklich das meine,
Herr Jesus, bist du gewiß?
Ist nicht eine wie eine,
wenn nicht irgend ein Biß
eine Schramme zurückläßt, Herr Jesus?

Kann es nicht sein, daß mein
Leben gar nicht dabei ist?
Daß es wo liegt und entzwei ist,
und der Regen regnet hinein
und steht drin und friert drin, Herr Jesus?

Since I never slept with anyone,
tell me: Have I been faithful to myself and to you?
And where was I when we sang?
Whom did I call, when I called on you?

IV.

My life went—Lord Jesus,
tell me where.
Did you see it run?
Am I in you?
Am I within you, Lord Jesus?

Just think, that's how life passes
with every day that comes and goes.
In the end, they all deny it existed,
no one has seen it or knows.
Was it my own, Lord Jesus?

Was it really my own,
are you sure?
Is not every woman the same unless
some bite mark and scar,
Lord Jesus, has been left on her?

Is it not possible that my life
is nowhere to be found?
That it is lying in a heap somewhere untold,
and the rain is pouring on it
and gathers in it, cold?

Probably Paris, January 1909

In der Certosa

Ein jeder aus der weißen Bruderschaft
vertraut sich pflanzend seinem kleinen Garten.
Auf jedem Beete steht, wer jeder sei.
Und Einer harrt in heimlichen Hoffahrten,
daß ihm im Mai
die ungestümen Blüten offenbarten
ein Bild von seiner unterdrückten Kraft.

Und seine Hände halten, wie erschlafft,
sein braunes Haupt, das schwer ist von den Säften,
die ungeduldig durch das Dunkel rollen,
und sein Gewand, das faltig, voll und wollen,
zu seinen Füßen fließt, ist stramm gestrafft
um seinen Armen, die, gleich starken Schäften,
die Hände tragen, welche träumen sollen.

Keine Miserere und kein Kyrie
will seine junge, runde Stimme ziehn,
vor keinem Fluche will sie fliehn:
sie ist kein Reh.
Sie ist ein Roß und bäumt sich im Gebiß,
und über Hürde, Hang und Hindernis
will sie ihn tragen, weit und weggewiß,
ganz ohne Sattel will tragen ihn.

Er aber sitzt, und unter den Gedanken
zerbrechen fast die breiten Handgelenke,
so schwer wird ihm der Sinn und immer schwerer.

Der Abend kommt, der sanfte Wiederkehrer,
ein Wind beginnt, die Wege werden leerer,
und Schatten sammeln sich im Talgesenke.

At the Cartusian Monastery
(The Book of Images, 1902/06– "The Second Book's
First Part")

Each among the white-dressed brotherhood
is bent on planting his little plot.
And each garden bed reflects the owner's life.
But there is one who hopes in secret pride
the month of May would at last profess
to him, with its reckless blossoming,
a glimpse of the strength he repressed.

And his hands hold up the tired
dark head filled with the juices of life
that pulse with impatience within;
and his robe lies in folds, woolen and wide,
and sags to his feet, but is tight
on his arms that resemble heavy beams,
with hands that are told to dream.

And his young, full voice refuses to give
a Miserere or a Kyrie,
and no curse can make the voice flee:
after all, she is not a doe, but is
a horse and rears behind teeth;
over hurdle, hill, and hindrance she hopes
to take him far, of her path she is sure;
and without a saddle she wants him to go.

But he sits, and amidst his thoughts
his sturdy wrists almost break apart,
so burdened he feels and the burden grows large.

The evening, this gentle pilgrim, returns,
a wind arises, the paths empty out,
with shadows collecting in the valley below.

Und wie ein Kahn, der an der Kette schwankt,
so wird der Garten ungewiß und hangt
wie windgewiegt auf lauter Dämmerung.
Wer löst ihn los? . . .

Der Frate ist so jung,
und langelang ist seine Mutter tot.
Er weiß von ihr: sie nannten sie La Stanca;
sie war ein Glas, ganz zart und klar.
Man botes einem, der es nach dem Trunk zerschlug
wie einen Krug.

So ist der Vater.
Und er hat sein Brot
als Meister in den roten Marmorbrüchen.
Und jede Wöchnerin in Pietrabianca
hat Furcht, daß er des Nachts mit seinen Flüchen
vorbei an ihrem Fenster kommt und droht.

Sein Sohn, den er der Donna Dolorosa
geweiht in einer Stunde wilder Not,
sinnt im Arkadenhofe der Certosa,
sinnt, wie umrauscht von rötlichen Gerüchen:
denn seine Blumen blühen alle rot.

And like a boat, dancing on its rope,
the garden grows dim and bobs on its noose
swayed by the winds of the evening.
Who'll cut it loose? . . .

The monk is still so young;
the mother long ago had died.
He knows they called her La Stanca;
she was like a glass, clear and fine.
They gave her to one who after he had
drunk his fill, had shattered and crushed
her like an empty jug.

Such is the father then.
And he makes a living by quarrying
red marble as a master workman.
Women big with child in Pietrabianca
are afraid that he with his cursing at night
comes up to their window to fight.

His son, whom he did dedicate
to the Donna Dolorosa when once desperately mad,
sits under the arcades of the Certosa
and ponders, enveloped as by reddish aromas:
since the flowers he planted bloom red.

*Cartusians are a contemplative religious order, whose members dress
in white cloaks and are dedicated to celibacy, solitude, and silence. In
his Florentine Diary, chronicling his stay in Florence between April
15 and the end of June 1898, Rilke had recorded a visit to a
Cartusian monastery, the Certosa des Val D'Ema. La Stanca (ital.)
is "the tired one"; Pietrabianca means "white stone"; and the Donna
Dolorosa is the Lady of Sorrows, a liturgical address for the Virgin*

Die Nonne

Die blonde Schwester trat in ihre Zelle
und schmiegte sich an sie: "Um meine Ruh
ist es geschehn. Ich wurde wie die Welle
und muß den fremden Meeren zu.
Und du bist klar. Du Heilige, du Helle,
mach mich wie du.
Gieb mir den Frieden, den du heimlich hast
und ohne Angst, so wie ihn keine hat,—
gieb mir die Rast;
daß ich ein Fels bin, wenn die Flut mich faßt,
und nicht ein Blatt."

Und leise neigte sich die Nonnenhafte—
nicht tief;
nur wie die Blüte horcht vom hohen Schafte,
wenn Wind sie rief.
Sie hatte längst die Gesten den Geländen
entlernt—die leise gebenden—
und fügte einen Kranz aus ihren Händen
und schenkte lächelnd ihn der Bebenden.

Und nach dem Schweigen waren sie sich nah;
so daß sie sich nicht dunkel fragen mußten
und sich nur klar das Letzte sagen mußten,
und das geschah:
"Sprich mir von Christo, dessen Braut du bist,
der dich erkor.
Und seiner Liebe, deren Laut du bist,

Mary. The poem contrasts the colors white and red, with white representing holiness and innocence, red human passion and transgression. Berlin-Schmargendorf, July 1899.

The Nun
(Christ—Eleven Visions, 1896/98)

The blond sister stepped into the cell
and sidled up to the other: "O my peace
is gone. I have become like a wave
compelled to drift toward foreign seas.
And you, you saintly one, are pure,
make me like you.
Give me this peace you hold inside
so without fear, the way none other has—
give me reprieve;
so I can be a rock when floods arrive,
and not a leaf."

And quietly the other sister bent to her,
not very low;
only like the blossom listens from above its stem,
when the wind called out.
She had long learned the gestures from the things
in nature—these gently surrendering ones—
and shaped her hands into a little wreath
and gave them smilingly to the trembling one.

And following the silence they drew close up;
of added questions neither one had need
and both did speak the very least
and understood:
"Talk to me about Christ whose bride you are,
who called you near.
And of his love, whose sound you are,

tu auf mein Ohr.
Laß mit mich wohnen
in seiner Trauer, deren Trost du bist
Du Leiserlöste, wie erlost du bist
aus Millionen."

Da küßte kühler sie die Priesterin
und sprach:
"Ich bin ja selbst an Gottes Anbeginn,
und dunkel ist mir meiner Sehnsucht Sinn—
Weit ist der Weg, und keiner weiß wohin,
doch sag ich dir, weil ich die Schwester bin:
Komm nach.
Mit einemmale wird dir Alles weit,
du langst dir nach.
Nur eine Weile geht noch aus der Zeit
die Angst dir nach.
Doch wenn du glaubst, so kann sie weit nicht mit
und sie wird lahm
und bleibt zuletzt.
Und wie es kam?
Das, was ich einmal litt,
lobpreis' ich jetzt.
Und Nächte giebt es, da die blasse Scham
entflieht,
da schenkt sich Jesus wie ein Lied
mir hin,
und meine Seele sieht,
daß ich ein Wunder bin,
das ihm geschieht."

Die Schwestern waren Brust an Brust gepreßt
und beide jung im Glühn des gleichen Scheines:

unlock my ear.
Allow me to make my dwelling
amidst his pain, whose solace you are!
You chosen one
from among a million."

The priestess coolly kissed her at that,
and said:
"But I am myself a novice with God
and dim is the longing of my eyes—
the path is far, no one knows its end,
but I tell you since a sister I am:
Do follow it.
All at once it becomes so clear,
and you reach for yourself in back.
For a little while only your fear lingers on
in your neck.
But if you have faith, it will lag behind
and grow lame
and altogether stay back.
And how did this come about?
What once caused me great pain for that
I now give praise.
And during nights when my passion pales
and flees,
it is then that Jesus gives himself like a song
to me,
and my soul understands
the wonder that I am
and is happening to him."

The sisters sat breast to breast immersed
and young amidst the same light's shine:

"Dann bin ich mit dem großen Leben Eines
und fühle tief: das ist das Hochzeitsfest,
und alle Krüge wurden Krüge Weines."

Da neigten die Mädchen sich Leib an Leib:
es war, als ob derselbe Sturm sie streifte
und sie umwob
und dann die Blonde hob
 in einen Sommer hoch, darin sie reifte
—zum Weib.

Denn sie küßte die Schwester mit fremdem Kuß
und lächelte fremd: "Vergieb,—ich muß.—
Weißt du noch von dem blonden Gespielen?
Und wir warfen nach weißen Zielen
schlanke Speere im alten Park:
Der ist jetzt stark."

Und da hielt die Nonne die Schwester nicht—
sah der Schwester nicht ins Gesicht,
ließ sie ganz langsam los,
wurde groß. . .

Die Blonde erschrak; denn kein Segen kam,
und bange bat sie: "So bist du mir gram?"
Die Heilige träumte: Ich hab dich lieb.

Und hielt der Schwester die Hände her,
leer,—
als flehte sie: gieb.

"Then I become one with all of life
and I deeply feel: this is the wedding feast
and all the jugs are filled with wine."

At this the girls moved their bodies close:
it was as if the same storm had touched
them both and tied them and wove
and then the blond one grew
in one summer, matured
to womanhood.

For she kissed the sister with a curious kiss
and oddly smiled: "Forgive, but I must tell.
Do you remember the boy with whom we played?
At white targets we were repeatedly aiming
the slender arrows in the old park:
He now is grown up."

And the nun immediately let go of her—
no longer did she look at her,
and slowly released her hold
and sat up . . .

The blond one flinched, for no blessing came,
and anxiously pleaded: "Do not be cross!"
The nun only thought: I still love you the same.

And she offered her hands to the sister again,
empty this time as if begging her:
give it up.

Probably Zoppot at the Baltic Sea in July 1898.

Das Jüngste Gericht

So erschrocken, wie sie nie erschraken,
ohne Ordnung, oft durchlocht und locker,
hocken sie in dem geborstnen Ocker
ihres Ackers, nicht von ihren Laken

abzubringen, die sie liebgewannen.
Aber Engel kommen an, um Öle
einzuträufeln in die trocknen Pfannen
und um jedem in die Achselhöhle

das zu legen, was er in dem Lärme
damals seines Lebens nicht entweihte;
denn dort hat es noch ein wenig Wärme,

daß es nicht des Herren Hand erkälte
oben, wenn er es aus jeder Seite
leise greift, zu fühlen, ob es gälte.

Das Jüngste Gericht
Aus den Blättern eines Mönchs

Sie werden Alle wie aus einem Bade
aus ihren mürben Grüften auferstehn;
denn alle glauben an das Wiedersehn,
und furchtbar ist ihr Glauben, ohne Gnade.

Sprich leise, Gott! Es könnte einer meinen,
daß die Posaune deiner Reiche rief;
und ihrem Ton ist keine Tiefe tief:

Judgment Day
(Of the New Poems' Other Part, 1908)

So terrified as never before and scattered,
frequently punctured and bruised,
they sit in the plowed orange of their plots
and are as if glued

to their blankets they have grown to love.
But there some angels arrive
who pour oil into dry pans and who shove
into the armpit of every one

the thing, which in the din of a life now gone,
they had not managed to desecrate,
and where their life still was warm

and would not chill the Lord's hand
when He began reaching for life in them
to see if it counted somewhat.

Paris, August 20, 1907; inspired by Michelangelo's mural in the Sistine Chapel.

Judgment Day—From the Notebooks of a Monk
(The Book of Images, 1902/06—"The Second Book's First Part")

They will all, as after taking a bath,
arise from their cavernous graves;
for all believe in another encounter,
and unbearable a faith that omits such a grace.

Whisper softly, Lord! Someone might think
that the trumpet of your coming has already blown;
for no depth exists too deep for it:

da steigen all Zeiten aus den Steinen,
und alle die Verschollenen erscheinen
in welken Leinen, brüchigen Gebeinen
und von der Schwere ihrer Schollen schief.
Das wird ein wunderliches Wiederkehren
in eine wunderliche Heimat sein;
auch die dich niemals kannten, werden schrein
und deine Größe wie ein Recht begehren:
wie Brot und Wein.

Allschauender, du kennst das wilde Bild,
das ich in meinem Dunkel zitternd dichte.
Durch dich kommt Alles, denn du bist das Tor,—
und Alles war in deinem Angesichte,
eh es in unserm sich verlor.
Du kennst das Bild vom riesigen Gerichte:

Ein Morgen ist es, doch aus einem Lichte,
das deine reife Liebe nie erschuf,
ein Rauschen ist es, nicht aus deinem Ruf,
ein Zittern, nicht von göttlichem Verzichte,
ein Schwanken, nicht in deinem Gleichgewichte.
Ein Rascheln ist und ein Zusammenraffen
in allen den geborstenen Gebäuden,
ein Sichentgelten und ein Sichvergeuden,
ein Sichbegatten und ein Sichbegaffen,
und ein Betasten aller alten Freuden
und aller Lüste welke Wiederkehr.
Und über Kirchen, die wie Wunden klaffen,
ziehn schwarze Vögel, die du nie erschaffen,
in irren Zügen hin und her.

So ringen sie, die lange Ausgeruhten,
und packen sich mit ihren nackten Zähnen

when all the past ages climb up from stones,
and all the departed appear
in crumpled-up cloth and with brittle bones,
bent by the weight of their tombs.
It will be a miraculous homecoming
to a country of miraculous shine;
even those who never knew you, will clamor
for your presence as if they were entitled to it:
clamor as for bread and wine.

Omniscient one, you know this wild image
that I in my blindness compose.
You are the gate; from you it all flows
what once was gathered before your face
and then disappeared before ours. You know
how this great judgment will go:

It happens at dawn, but in a light
that never arose on account of you,
a howling there is, not created by you,
a trembling, but not from divine resolve,
a tumbling that's not in balance with you.
A rustling there is and a gathering
in all the buildings now swept,
a reserving of oneself and a splurging,
a mating and a looking at,
and a touching of all the former joys
and the worn-out return of desires.
And over the churches, gaping like wounds,
there flit black birds, none created by you,
flying furiously back and forth.

Thus they struggle, the long rested,
with their naked teeth exposed, get up

und werden bange, weil sie nicht mehr bluten,
und suchen, wo die Augenbecher gähnen,
mit kalten Fingern nach den toten Tränen.
Und werden müde. Wenige Minuten
nach ihrem Morgen bricht ihr Abend ein.
Sie werden ernst und lassen sich allein
und sind bereit, im Sturme aufzusteigen,
wenn sich auf deiner Liebe heitrem Wein
die dunklen Tropfen deines Zornes zeigen,
um deinem Urteil nah zu sein.
Und da beginnt es, nach dem großen Schrein:
das übergroße fürchterliche Schweigen.

Sie sitzen all wie vor schwarzen Türen
in einem Licht, das sie, wie mit Geschwüren,
mit vielen grellen Flecken übersät.
Und wachsend wird der Abend alt und spät.
Und Nächte fallen dann in großen Stücken
auf ihre Hände und auf ihren Rücken,
der wankend sich mit schwarzer Last belädt.
Sie warten lange. Ihre Schultern schwanken
unter dem Drucke wie ein dunkles Meer,
sie sitzen, wie versunken in Gedanken,
und sind doch leer.
Was stützen sie die Stirnen?
Ihre Gehirne denken irgendwo
tief in der Erde, eingefallen, faltig:
Die ganze alte Erde denkt gewaltig,
und ihre großen Bäume rauschen so.

Allschauender, gedenkst du dieses bleichen
und bangen Bildes, das nicht seinesgleichen
unter den Bildern deines Willens hat?
Hast du nicht Angst vor dieser stummen Stadt,

and fret since they no longer do bleed,
and search in their hollow eye sockets
for tears with hands that freeze.
They are weary. Only minutes past dawn
they are again covered by dusk.
They grow serious and surrender
and have resolved to scramble up,
when suddenly on the joyous surface of your love,
—so as to be nearer your verdict,
pearl up the dark drops of your wrath.
And then, after all this bustling and noise,
the terrible towering silence arrives.

They all sit as before black openings
in a light that clothes them with numerous
blotches so bright and like tumors.
And the evening is prolonged and grows old.
And the nights burst into big chunks
that drop upon their hands and their back,
bearing the pitch-dark weight.
They wait. Their shoulders sag
under the force of the tide,
and they sit about as if pondering,
but are empty inside.
Why would they prop their heads?
Their brains have gone out to roam
underground, shriveled up and squeezed:
Now this earth is steeped into their ponderings
with sounds only coming from trees.

Omniscient one, do you give any thought
to this daunting and worrisome scene,
unmatched by all the others you did draft?
Are you not troubled by this silent city,

die, an dir hangend wie ein welkes Blatt,
sich heben will zu deines Zornes Zeichen?
O, greife allen Tagen in die Speichen,
daß sie zu bald nicht diesem Ende nahen,—
vielleicht gelingt es dir noch auszuweichen
dem großen Schweigen, das wir beide sahen.
Vielleicht kannst du noch einen aus uns heben,
der diesem fürchterlichen Wiederleben
den Sinn, die Sehnsucht und die Seele nimmt,
einen, der bis in seinen Grund ergrimmt
und dennoch froh, durch alle Dinge schwimmt,
der Kräfte unbekümmerter Verbraucher,
der sich auf allen Saiten geigt
und unversehrt als unerkannter Taucher
in alle Tode niedersteigt.
. . . Oder, wie hoffst du diesen Tag zu tragen,
der länger ist als aller Tage Längen,
mit seines Schweigens schrecklichen Gesängen,
wenn dann die Engel sind, wie lauter Fragen,
mit ihrem schauerlichen Flügelschlagen
umdrängen?
Sieh, wie sie zitternd in den Schwingen hängen
und dir mit hunderttausend Augen klagen,
und ihres sanften Liedes Stimmen wagen
sich aus den vielen wirren Übergängen
nicht mehr zu heben zu den klaren Klängen.
Und wenn die Greise mit den breiten Bärten,
die dich berieten bei den besten Siegen,
nur leise ihre weißen Häupter wiegen,
und wenn die Frauen, die den Sohn dir nährten
und die von ihm Verführten, die Gefährten,
und alle Jungfraun, die sich ihm gewährten:
die lichten Birken deiner dunklen Gärten,—
wer soll dir helfen, wenn sie alle schwiegen?

clinging to you like a withering leaf,
but ready to erupt with your wrath?
O Lord, reach into the twirling spokes
of days headed toward this end—
perhaps you can avert the imminent
silence we both see approach.
Perhaps you could raise from among us one
who takes from this dreadful resurrection
the meaning, purpose, and general direction,
one who is deeply touched by it all
yet retains serenity overall,
an unmoved partaker of every thing,
played by and playing every string,
and diving safely and secretly
toward each death there is.
How else would you expect to endure
this day, longer than any before,
with its terrible periods of silences,
and with the angels, like question marks, pressing
around you and relentlessly flapping
their wings?
See, they hang in the air and quiver
and plead with a hundred thousand eyes;
the voices of their gentle song cannot rise
from the tangled transitions so as to intone
a clear and harmonious song.
And see, the old men with beards so wide,
who used to advise you for victory's sake,
are quietly tilting their heads;
and see the women who nursed your son,
and those drawn to him who followed along,
and virgins, who only knew one:
these are the birches in your dark yard and your light—
who else might help you if they all keep quiet?

Und nur dein Sohn erhübe sich unter denen,
welche sitzen um deinen Thron.
Grübe sich deine Stimme dann in sein Herz?
Sagte dein einsamer Schmerz dann:
Sohn!
Suchtest du dann das Angesicht
dessen, der das Gericht gerufen,
dein Gericht und deinen Thron:
Sohn!
Hießest du, Vater, dann deinen Erben,
leise begleitet von Magdalenen,
niedersteigen zu jenen,
die sich sehnen, wieder zu sterben?

Das wäre dein letzter Königserlaß,
die letzte Huld und der letzte Haß.
Aber dann käme Alles zu Ruh:
der Himmel und das Gericht und du.
Alle Gewänder des Rätsels der Welt,
das sich so lange verschleiert hält,
fallen mit dieser Spange.
. . . Doch mir ist bange. . .

Allschauender, sieh, wie mir bange ist,
miß meine Qual!
Mir ist bange, daß du schon lange vergangen bist.
Als du zum erstenmal
in deinem Alleserfassen
das Bild dieses blassen
Gerichtes sahst,
dem du dich hülflos nahst, Allschauender.
Bist du damals entflohn?
Wohin?

And only your son would stand up from among
those seated around your throne.
Would your voice then aim at his heart?
And your lonely pain cry:
Son!
Would you then search for his eyes,
for the one who convened the court,
your court and your throne, crying:
Son!
Would you, Father, then command
that your heir, accompanied by women, descend,
to those who long
to die once more?

That would be your final edict,
both the ultimate grace and the ultimate wrath.
And then everything would be appeased:
the heavens and all righteousness and you.
All the covers that veil
the perpetual mystery of the world,
would drop at once by this deed.
But I am afraid.

Omniscient one, see how I fret
and take stock of my pain!
I am worried that long ago
you left, when first you perceived
the image of this dismal day
of judgment,
helplessly.
Did you escape then?
Whereto?
No one could beseech

Vertrauender
kann keiner dir kommen
als ich,
der ich dich
nicht zum Lohn
verraten will wie alle Frommen.
Ich will nur, weil ich verborgen bin
und müde wie du, noch müder vielleicht,
und weil meine Angst vor dem großen Gericht
deiner gleicht,
will ich mich dicht,
Gesicht bei Gesicht,
an dich heften;
mit einigen Kräften
werden wir wehren dem großen Rade,
über welches die mächtigen Wasser gehn,
die rauschen und schnauben—
denn: wehe, sie werden auferstehn.
So ist ihr Glauben: groß und ohne Gnade.

you more innocently
than me,
for I would not
turn you in for a reward,
as all the pious do.
Since I am in hiding
and tired like you, perhaps more,
and since my fear of the day of judgment
resembles yours,
I only want to pin myself,
cheek to cheek,
unto you;
then with joint force
we would stem the great wheel,
spun by the mighty waters
with its growling roar—
Woe, if they come back to life and are raised.
Yes, that's their faith: big, without grace.

The first stanzas are most likely based on paintings of the Last Judgment. Among them are Michelangelo's mural in the Sistine Chapel and paintings by Bonamico, a fourteenth century painter, whom Rilke called the "old master of the 'Triumph of Death' and of the 'Last Judgment'." Rilke's poem appears to reflect on the depictions of the dead by Georg Heym's paintings, such as The Dead on the Mountain, The Morgue, Styx, and Clouds. Berlin-Schmargendorf, July 1899.

V. Von der Armut

Die Stimmen—Titelblatt

Die Reichen und Glücklichen haben gutschweigen,
niemand will wissen was sie sind.
Aber die Dürftigen müssen sich zeigen,
müssen sagen: ich bin blind
oder: ich bin im Begriff es zu werden
oder: es geht mir nicht gut auf Erden
oder: ich habe ein krankes Kind
oder: da bin ich zusammengefügt. . .

Und vielleicht, daß das gar nicht genügt.

Und weil alle sonst, wie an Dingen,
an ihnen vorbeigehn, müssen sie singen.

Und da hört man noch guten Gesang.

Freilich die Menschen sind seltsam; sie hören
lieber Kastraten in Knabenchören.

Aber Gott selber kommt und bleibt lang
wenn ihn diese Beschnittenen stören.

V. On Poverty

Voices—Title Page

(The Book of Images, 1902/1906– "The Second Book's
Second Part")

It's easy for the rich and happy ones to keep quiet,
for who needs to know what they are.
But the poor have a need to display
themselves and need to say: I am blind,
or: I am in the process of becoming it
or: it is not well with me
or: I have a sick child
or: here is where I manage . . .

But even that may not suffice.

And since they would be passed over, otherwise,
so easily like things, they are compelled to sing.

And so, one can still hear good songs there.

Of course, people are strange; they prefer
to listen to eunuchs in boy choirs.

But God is personally present and listens at length
when these other eunuchs seek attention from Him.

*Paris, May 1906; the "Voices" is a cycle of nine poems on the mar-
ginalized, oppressed, and poor.*

Wort-Armut*

Ich fürchte mich so vor der Menschen Wort.
Sie sprechen alles so deutlich aus:
Und dieses heißt Hund und jenes heißt Haus,
und hier ist Beginn und das Ende ist dort.

Mich bangt auch ihr Sinn, ihr Spiel mit dem Spott,
sie wissen alles, was wird und war;
kein Berg ist ihnen mehr wunderbar;
ihr Garten und Gut grenzt grade an Gott.

Ich will immer warnen und wehren: Bleibt fern.
Die Dinge singen hör ich so gern.
Ihr rührt sie an: sie sind starr und stumm.
 Ihr bringt mir alle die Dinge um.

Todes-Erfahrung

Wir wissen nichts von diesem Hingehn, das
nicht mit uns teilt. Wir haben keinen Grund,
Bewunderung und Liebe oder Haß
dem Tod zu zeigen, den ein Maskenmund

Poverty of Words*
(In Celebration of Me, 1909)

I am so afraid of people's words.
They describe so distinctly everything:
And this they call dog and that they call house,
here the start and there the end.

I worry about their mockery with words,
they know everything, what will be, what was;
no mountain is still miraculous;
and their house and yard lead right up to God.

I want to warn and object: Let the things be!
I enjoy listening to the sound they are making.
But you always touch: and they hush and stand still.
That's how you kill.

The poem marks Rilke's increasing skepticism of a poetic language that relies on traditional symbol, form, and narrative since such language trivialized the mystery of life and God. In his March 1898 lecture on modern lyric, his 1898 essay "On the Melody of Things," and his Florentine Diary, Rilke proposes a language that employs objects, landscapes, and shapes, along with sound, rhythm, and the setting-free of various levels of connotation so as to suggest an "état d'âme." Thereby, subject matter and content are merely used as a pretext to express the soul's most subtle feelings and sensations. Berlin-Wilmersdorf, November 1898.

Death Experience
(New Poems, 1907)

We know nothing of this departing
that has never been shared. But no reason exists
to display admiration and love, or hate for Death
since his mouth wears a mask

tragischer Klage wunderlich entstellt.
Noch ist die Welt voll Rollen, die wir spielen.
Solang wir sorgen, ob wir auch gefielen,
spielt auch der Tod, obwohl er nicht gefällt.

Doch als du gingst, da brach in diese Bühne
ein Streifen Wirklichkeit durch jenen Spalt
durch den du hingingst: Grün wirklicher Grüne,
wirklicher Sonnenschein, wirklicher Wald.

Wir spielen weiter. Bang und schwer Erlerntes
hersagend und Gebärden dann und wann
aufhebend; aber dein von uns entferntes,
aus unserm Stück entrücktes Dasein kann

uns manchmal überkommen, wie ein Wissen
von jener Wirklichkeit sich niedersenkend,
so daß wir eine Weile hingerissen
das Leben spielen, nicht an Beifall denkend.

Der Gefangene

I.

Meine Hand hat nur noch eine
Gebärde, mit der sie verscheucht;
auf die alten Steine
fällt es aus Felsen feucht.

and is strangely distorted by woeful complaints.
The world is full of the roles we play;
but as long as we worry about how to please,
we permit Death to be playing his.

Then with your coming there burst on stage
as through a crack, a smidgeon of truth;
you walked in it: it was truest hue
of green, of sunshine, of woods.

And we continue as actors, reciting
what we memorized with the gestures we learned.
Though your presence, which we removed
from our plot of spurious living,

can sometimes break upon us in a sudden flash
of another reality, so that swept up we abruptly pause
briefly and engage in the play of life
and do not seek applause.

*Written in recognition of the first anniversary of the death of
Countess Luise Schwerin on January 24, 1906, to her sister Alice
Faehndrich. Capri, January 24, 1907.*

The Prisoner
(New Poems, 1907)

I.

My hand has only one gesture left
with which to brush away;
and the brushed-away drops
onto stone old and wet.

Ich höre nur dieses Klopfen
und mein Herz hält Schritt
mit dem Gehen der Tropfen
und vergeht damit.

Tropften sie doch schneller,
käme doch wieder ein Tier.
Irgendwo war es heller—.
Aber was wissen wir.

II.

Denk dir, das was jetzt Himmel ist und Wind,
Luft deinem Mund und deinem Auge Helle,
das würde Stein bis um die kleine Stelle
an der dein Herz und deine Hände sind.

Und was jetzt in dir morgen heißt und: dann
und: späterhin und nächstes Jahr und weiter—
das würde wund in dir und voller Eiter
und schwäre nur und bräche nicht mehr an.

Und das was war, das wäre irre und
raste in dir herum, den lieben Mund
der niemals lachte, schäumend von Gelächter.

Und das was Gott war, wäre nur dein Wächter
und stopfte boshaft in das letzte Loch
ein schmutziges Auge. Und du lebtest doch

I can hear only this dropping,
and the knocking of my heart
keeps pace with the drops' beat
and disappears with it.

If only the drops would run faster,
if only some animal returned.
It would make a difference somehow—.
But, what do I know.

II.

Just imagine, that which is now wind and sky,
air for breathing and light to your eye,
would have turned to stone but for the small part
that are your hands and heart.

And that which is called tomorrow in you,
and: later on and next year and further—
would have become inflamed and pus-filled
and kept on festering and would not heal.

And all your past would go wild in you
and race about, and your gentle mouth
without smile, would be foaming with laughter.

And all that's your God would be only the guard,
stuffing with malice into the last hole
one dirty eye. And you'd still be alive.

Meudon, probably spring of 1906

Der Alchimist

Seltsam verlächelnd schob der Laborant
den Kolben fort, der halbberuhigt rauchte.
Er wußte jetzt, was er noch brauchte,
damit der sehr erlauchte Gegenstand

da drin entstände. Zeiten brauchte er,
Jahrtausende für sich und diese Birne
in der es brodelte; im Hirn Gestirne
und im Bewußtsein mindestens das Meer.

Das Ungeheuere, das er gewollt,
er ließ es los in dieser Nacht. Es kehrte
zurück zu Gott und in sein altes Maß;

er aber, lallend wie ein Trunkenbold,
lag über dem Geheimfach und begehrte
den Brocken Gold, den er besaß.

Aus dem Leben eines Heiligen

Er kannte Ängste, deren Eingang schon
wie Sterben war und nicht zu überstehen.
Sein Herz erlernte, langsam durchzugehen;
er zog es groß wie einen Sohn.

Und namenlose Nöte kannte er,
finster und ohne Morgen wie Verschläge;
und seine Seele gab er folgsam her,
da sie erwachsen war, auf daß sie läge

The Alchemist
(Of the New Poems' Other Part, 1908)

Strangely asmile the alchemist pushes aside
the bottle smoking semi-appeased.
He knew now of what he still had need
so the highly prized object could form.

Of time there was need, of millennia maybe,
for himself and for this pear-shaped simmering glass;
for his brains he still was in need of the stars
and for self-reflection he needed the sea.

But the incomprehensible that he had so desired,
he let slip away that night. And in turn,
it went back to God, to its original form;

while he, still babbling like a drunken fool,
lay over the secret coffer and lusted
for the lump of gold he already owned.

Paris, August 1907

From the Life of a Saint
(Of the New Poems' Other Part, 1908)

He knew of fears that resembled death,
dreadfully hard to survive.
His heart was beginning to walk through them;
he raised it like a child.

He knew these dark nights, the nameless
impasses, without windows of light;
and obediently he released his soul,
matured now, so as to recline

bei ihrem Bräutigam und Herrn; und blieb
allein zurück an einem solchen Orte,
wo das Alleinsein alles übertrieb,
und wohnte weit und wollte niemals Worte.

Aber dafür, nach Zeit und Zeit, erfuhr
er auch das Glück, sich in die eignen Hände,
damit er eine Zärtlichkeit empfände,
zu legen wie die ganze Kreatur.

Der Stylit

Völker schlugen über ihm zusammen,
die er küren durfte und verdammen;
und erratend, daß er sich verlor,
klomm er aus dem Volksgeruch mit klammen
Händen einen Säulenschaft empor,

der noch immer stieg und nichts mehr hob,
und begann, allein auf seiner Fläche,
ganz von vorne seine eigne Schwäche
zu vergleichen mit des Herren Lob;

und da war kein Ende: er verglich;
und der Andre wurde immer größer.
Und die Hirten, Ackerbauer, Flößer
sahn ihn klein und außer sich

with her groom and Lord; he sought
for himself a lonely spot,
where being alone was paramount,
while refraining from saying a word.

And after many, many trials like this,
he could experience the joy of releasing
himself with all of his being
as a gentle caress.

*The poem is one of eight in a series dealing with people's estrangement
from each other and the large city's oppressive force; among those fea-
tured in the series are the mentally ill, beggars, morgue workers, and
a blind man. Similarities in theme and style exist with Bauedelaire's
Fleurs de Mal. Paris, August 5-September 5, 1907.*

The Stylite
(Of the New Poems' Other Part, 1908)

Whole nations would collide above his head
which he was entitled to bless or curse;
and intent on learning to surrender it all,
he clambered away from the people's scent
up a pillar with rigid hands—

rising up high and without support,
and began, alone on the pillar's plateau,
to take stock of his sins going back to the start
and releasing them unto the Lord;

there was no end: he took stock and compared;
the other became ever brighter and great.
And the shepherds and farmers and raftsmen below
could observe him grow meek, in disarray

immer mit dem ganzen Himmel reden,
eingeregnet manchmal, manchmal licht;
und sein Heulen stürzte sich auf jeden,
so als heulte er ihm ins Gesicht.
Doch er sah seit Jahren nicht,

wie der Menge Drängen und Verlauf
unten unaufhörlich sich ergänzte,
und das Blanke an den Fürsten glänzte
lange nicht so hoch hinauf.

Aber wenn er oben, fast verdammt
und von ihrem Widerstand zerschunden,
einsam mit verzweifeltem Geschreie
schüttelte die täglichen Dämonen:
fielen langsam auf die erste Reihe
schwer und ungeschickt aus seinen Wunden
große Würmer in die offnen Kronen
und vermehrten sich im Samt.

arguing and talking with the heavens above,
rainy some days and others fair;
and his crying descended on each of them,
like a cry aimed straight at their head.
And over the years, he did separate

from the push and pull of the people below
and how it replenished perpetually,
and the polished gear of the noblemen
did not manage to rise to his eyes.

But when up there, almost exiled
and by people's stubbornness bruised,
he shook with his many cries of despair
all alone the daily demons off:
there slowly dropped from his wounds
heavy, clumsily onto the first row
the biggest worms into open crowns
and bred in the velvety clothes.

Based on Simeon Stylites (c. 390-459), who was the first and most famous of the pillar hermits. Simeon was a Cilician shepherd and spent several of his teen years in a monastery at Heliodorus, where he practiced such severe mortifications that he was dismissed from there. He then became a hermit at the foot of a mountain near Antioch and after three years moved to the top of the mountain, where word of his holiness began to attract huge crowds. To escape them in 423, he erected a ten-foot-high pillar, on which he lived, and which he gradually increased to 60 or 70 feet. Here, never descending until his death, he daily preached and exhorted to greater holiness his steady stream of listeners, which included commoners as well as prelates and emperors. The earliest depictions of him stem from the fifth century, and his relics, column, and image instantly became objects of popular veneration. Paris, early summer 1908.

Sankt Sebastian

Wie ein Liegender so steht er; ganz
hingehalten von dem großen Willen.
Weitentrückt wie Mütter, wenn sie stillen,
und in sich gebunden wie ein Kranz.

Und die Pfeile kommen: jetzt und jetzt
und als sprängen sie aus seinen Lenden,
eisern bebend mit den freien Enden.
Doch er lächelt dunkel, unverletzt.

Einmal nur wird seine Trauer groß,
und die Augen liegen schmerzlich bloß,
bis sie etwas leugnen, wie Geringes,
und als ließen sie verächtlich los
die Vernichter eines schönen Dinges.

St. Sebastian
(New Poems, 1907)

As if lying down, he is standing there;
completely sustained by an inner strength.
Far removed like mothers who are nursing,
entwined in himself like a wreath.

And the arrows are hitting: now and again,
as if erupting from his sides,
quivering intensely at the ends.
But he, unmoved, darkly smiles.

Just once his sadness stings,
and his eyes grow painfully large
until they reject, as one would grime,
and relinquish with utter disdain
the murderers of a beautiful thing.

*According to legend, Sebastian became a soldier in the Roman army
in 283 and made numerous converts to the Christian faith. Sebastian
was named captain in the praetorian guards by Emperor Diocletian,
and later by Emperor Maximian when Diocletian went to the East,
neither knowing that Sebastian was a Christian. When it was discov-
ered during Maximian's persecution of Christians, Sebastian was
ordered executed and was shot with arrows. But when the widow of
St. Castulus went to recover the body, she found him still alive and
nursed him back to health. Soon thereafter Sebastian intercepted the
Emperor and denounced his cruelty, whereupon he was beaten to death
at the Emperor's orders. Sebastian was venerated as a martyr saint in
Milan as early as during Ambrose's time in the late fourth century.
Many Renaissance artists depicted St. Sebastian's being shot with
arrows, including Botticelli, whose painting probably inspired Rilke
when seeing it in the Kaiser-Friedrich-Museum, Berlin. Meudon, winter 1905-06.*

Sankt Christopherus

Die große Kraft will für den Größten sein.
Nun hoffte er, ihm endlich hier zu dienen
an dieses Flusses Furt; er kam von zwein
berühmten Herren, die ihm klein erschienen,
und ließ sich dringend mit dem dritten ein:

den er nicht kannte; den er durch Gebet
und Fastenzeiten nicht auf sich genommen,
doch der im Ruf steht, jedem nachzukommen
der alles läßt und für ihn geht.

So trat er täglich durch den vollen Fluß—
Ahnherr der Brücken, welche steinern schreiten,—
und war erfahren auf den beiden Seiten
und fühlte jeden, der hinüber muß.

Und ruhte nachts in dem geringen Haus,
gefaßt zu handeln, jeder Stimme inne,
und atmete die Mühe mächtig aus,
genießend das Geräumige seiner Sinne.

Dann rief es einmal, dünn und hoch: ein Kind.
Er hob sich groß, daß er es überführe;
doch wissend, wie die Kinder ängstlich sind,
trat er ganz eingeschränkt aus seiner Türe
und bückte sich—: und draußen war Nachtwind.

Er murmelte: Was sollte auch ein Kind. . .?
nahm sich zurück mit einem großen Schritte
und lag in Frieden und entschlief geschwind.
Aber da war es wieder, voller Bitte.
Er spähte wieder—: draußen war Nachtwind.

St. Christopher
(Poems 1906-1926)

Great strength wants to serve the Almighty.
And so he, the strong, hoped to serve Him here
by the river. He had been serving before
two noble men, who appeared to him now small,
for his present dealings were with a third:

whom he didn't know; whom he never had
sought in prayer and fasting, yet who
was known to come to anyone willing
to leave things behind and walk in His stead.

Thus daily, through the river he stomped—
as master of bridges that had started to walk,—
and was well familiar with both of its banks
and carried whoever across.

At night he slept in a simple house,
prepared to get up, of calls aware,
exhaling the labor's strain mightily
and enjoying the freedom he had.

And one time he heard the call of a child.
And he raised himself to carry it;
yet fully aware of the children's fright
of giants like him, he crouched and stepped out—
but there in the night was just wind.

He mumbled: A child at this hour, no way!
and returned to the house with a mighty stride
and laid down in peace and went back to sleep.
But again, the child's voice returned like a plea.
He looked—; as before, just the wind.

Da ist doch keiner, oder bin ich blind?
warf er sich vor und ging noch einmal schlafen,
bis ihn dieselben Laute zwingend lind
noch einmal im verdeckten Innern trafen:
Er kam gewaltig:
                            draußen war ein Kind.

Der Auszug des Verlorenen Sohnes

Nun fortzugehn von alledem Verworrnen,
das unser ist und uns doch nicht gehört,
das, wie das Wasser in den alten Bornen,
uns zitternd spiegelt und das Bild zerstört;
von allem diesen, das sich wie die Dornen
noch einmal an uns anhängt—fortzugehn
und Das und Den,
die man schon nicht mehr sah
(so täglich waren sie und so gewöhnlich),
auf einmal anzuschauen: sanft, versöhnlich
und wie an einem Anfang und von nah;

Nobody there, am I blind? he said,
reproaching himself, and went back to bed;
but the same voice now with gentle force
struck within his heart: and he with might
responded:

                    there was a child.

*According to church tradition, Christopher was a giant of the third
century who made his living carrying people across a river. He tried to
find someone more powerful than himself and decided this could only
be Christ, since the devil feared the Savior. One day one of his pas-
sengers was a small child who grew so heavy as they were crossing the
river that he feared they both would drown. The child then revealed
himself as Christ, whose heaviness was caused by his carrying the
weight of the world. Christopher means Christ-bearer, and he is venerated in both East and West. In the Roman Catholic Church he is
regarded as the patron saint of travelers. For centuries paintings, icons,
and amulets have depicted him with a heavy walking stick in hand
carrying the Christ child seated on his shoulders. Paris, April 1913.*

Departure of the Prodigal Son
(New Poems, 1907)

To leave behind all this entangled mess
that is ours and that we do not even possess;
all that mirrors us like water in old wells
distorting and disfiguring our face;
to leave behind all that clings
to us as with thorns over and over again—
these somethings and someones
we don't even notice anymore
(that's how banal and average they are),
and to take another look at them: gently, and to reconcile,
as when making a fresh start, and to step close up;

und ahnend einzusehn, wie unpersönlich,
wie über alle hin das Leid geschah,
von dem die Kindheit voll war bis zum Rand—:
Und dann noch fortzugehen, Hand aus Hand,
als ob man ein Geheiltes neu zerrisse,
und fortzugehn: wohin? Ins Ungewisse,
weit in ein unverwandtes warmes Land,
das hinter allem Handeln wie Kulisse
gleichgültig sein wird: Garten oder Wand;
und fortzugehn: warum? Aus Drang, aus Artung,
aus Ungeduld, aus dunkler Erwartung,
aus Unverständlichkeit und Unverstand:

Dies alles auf sich nehmen und vergebens
vielleicht Gehaltnes fallen lassen, um
allein zu sterben, wissend nicht warum—

Ist das der Eingang eines neuen Lebens?—

and to recognize instinctively the pain
that had undeservedly happened to them
from early childhood on—:
And then still to depart and let go,
as if tearing open a wound freshly healed,
and to leave: whereto? Into uncertainty,
into a strange land that feels warm and will be
backdrop and indifferent to our doings
like garden and wall; why? Out of desire or design,
out of impatience or hidden expectation,
out of ignorance or lack of explanation.

To take up one's cross and to release,
perhaps in vain, what one had been holding so tight
and to die alone, though unsure of the reasons—

Is this not entering new life?

*The poem takes its title from the parable of the Prodigal Son in Luke
15:11-32, but instead of celebrating the son's return, it focuses on his
renewed departure. Rilke alludes to two sayings of Jesus in the previous chapter of Luke: "Whoever comes to me and does not hate father
and mother, wife and children, brothers and sisters, yes, and even life
itself, cannot be my disciple. Whoever does not carry the cross and follow me cannot be my disciple" (Luke 14:26-27, NRSV); and "none
of you can become my disciple if you do not give up all your possessions" (Luke 14:33; NRSV). Rilke may have been inspired by the
fourteenth-century wall hanging of the Prodigal Son in the cathedral
of Marburg. Written in Paris, June 1906.*